FOLLOWING THE SYNAGOGUE SERVICE

By the same Author

Understanding the Synagogue Service (1974)
A Samaritan Chronicle (1982)
Festival Adventure (1982)
Yizkor (1983)
Understanding the High Holyday Services (1983)
Horizons of Jewish Prayer (1986)
Moments of Insight (1989)
Blessed Are You (1993)
Prayer and Penitence (1994)
1001 Questions and Answers on Pesach (1996)
*1001 Questions and Answers on Rosh Hashanah
        and Yom Kippur* (1997)

Following The Synagogue Service

A Guide to the Weekday and Shabbat Services

By Jeffrey M Cohen

With a Foreword by the Emeritus Chief Rabbi, Lord Jakobovits

Gnesia Publications

Published in Great Britain in 1997 by
Gnesia Publications
69, London Road, Stanmore, Middx. HA7 4PA
telephone: 0181 954 2877
fax: 0181 385 7124
e-mail: Jeffrey@yonah.demon.co.uk

Hebrew and English typesetting:
Bernard Gerstein, Borehamwood, Herts.

Printed by:
The Nuffield Press
Abingdon, Oxon.

ISBN 0-946000-01-8

For Janice

This book is dedicated by
Thelma and Norman Epstein
to the sacred memory of
their beloved daughter Janice,
who died on 16th May 1990.

May her dear soul rest in peace

תְּהִי נִשְׁמָתָה צְרוּרָה בִּצְרוֹר הַחַיִּים

Contents

Contents

Foreword

Our Sages refer to Prayer as 'Service of the Heart'. But the heart cannot work properly unless the brain functions to stimulate and control its operation. In the physiology of Prayer, too, the mind plays as vital a role as the heart. If we do not comprehend the spiritual mechanics and inner meaning of our superb prayers, they cannot serve their intended purpose as the ladder linking heaven and earth for the 'ascent of man to God' and as the vehicle of this response to man's needs. Hence the emphasis in Jewish law on the supreme importance of *kavanah,* or proper devotion and understanding, in the recitation of our prayers.

Avodah (worship) is placed between *Torah* (Jewish learning) and *gemilut chasadim* (deeds of charity) as the central pillar among the three foundations sustaining Jewish life. This volume is a valuable attempt to assist the worshipper in the sound construction of this central pillar. It is a useful response to the widespread complaint made by many people attending synagogue that they 'cannot follow the service'.

Rabbi Dr Jeffrey Cohen adorns the Anglo-Jewish ministry as one of its most scholarly and creative members. His books can now be found in many Jewish homes here and abroad, and he has helped to generate a refreshingly new esteem for Anglo-Jewish letters. Combining sound learning with grace of expression, his works are both substantial and attractive.

This considerably expanded edition includes several new features on more general liturgical themes, including the role of the *Chazan* and the rabbi in the synagogue, the efficacy of prayer in Jewish thought, the prayer obligations of women and the needs of those who cannot read Hebrew.

May the prayers enhanced by this work find acceptance before Him Who hearkens to prayer.

Emeritus Chief Rabbi, Lord Jakobovits

Preface

This book is a thoroughly revised and expanded version of my first book, *Understanding the Synagogue Service*, published in Glasgow in 1974 with a Foreword by the then Chief Rabbi, Dr (now Lord) Immanuel Jakobovits. It is a great privilege for me that Lord Jakobovits has graciously accepted my invitation to him to write an up-dated Foreword for this edition.

The original edition proved most popular, and the idea of re-issuing it took shape as a result of the regular requests that have been made for the book by booksellers and individuals. While the new Centenary edition of the *Singer's Prayer Book* and the *ArtScroll Siddur* have certainly made the *Siddur* more user-friendly, yet, I am assured, there is no substitute for a handbook which provides, in compact form, all the help, guidance and information required by worshippers who are not *au fait* with the mechanics of the synagogue, its services and its prayer book.

This new edition should prove especially helpful to returnees to the synagogue, daunted after a lengthy period of absence, during which they had forgotten how to follow the service, how to find their way around the *Siddur*, how to put on their *Tefillin*, what to do when called-up, and so on. It is also geared to those who are, at the same time, seeking some general background information regarding the history, meaning and significance of the main prayers and the ritual objects used in the synagogue, as well as on the role of the synagogue officials. In this respect, it should also be of help to students in Jewish schools and Hebrew classes. For those who cannot read Hebrew, I have also included a key to Hebrew reading, as well as a transliterated section, with selected prayers and hymns, to enable them to absorb the essential ethos of the liturgy, and also to mitigate their embarrassment in synagogue.

It is my hope that this book will help to clarify much of the mystery and complexity that, quite unnecessarily, is associated with the services. Regular attendance is, in the final analysis, the only means to achieve total familiarity. This book is not intended to replace that requirement.

I should like to thank all those who have offered assistance and suggestions in the production of this book, especially Mr Harold Harris, who oversaw every stage of its production and produced the *Tefillin*

Preface

photographs, Mrs Ruth Lanning who typed the text, Mr Bernard Gerstein, who undertook the responsibility for the insertion of the Hebrew text, layout and design, and who offered invaluable editorial suggestions, Mr James Proops, who kindly modelled for the *Tefillin* photographs, as well as to Mr Dan Rubinstein, the cover artist. I also acknowledge with thanks permission granted to me by the *Jewish Chronicle* (London) to include four articles from my current monthly series "Pearls of Prayer".

This book would not have appeared were it not for the great interest shown in it by Thelma and Norman Epstein, and their generosity in offsetting the cost of its production in memory of their beloved Janice who was so tragically taken from them in a motor accident. We wish them and their family only comfort and happiness in the future.

As always, I thank my dear wife, Gloria, for her encouragement of all my spiritual and literary endeavours. Special appreciation to her, and to my children and lovely grandchildren, for giving me the ingredient of joy which, according to the psalmist, is essential for the true service of God.

Jeffrey M Cohen
London, 1997

Page references are provided in the left-hand margin of the section of this book which describes the Synagogue services. Of the two page references, the first refers to *The Authorised Daily (Singer's) Prayer Book* (Centenary edition, London 1990). The second reference, in square brackets, is to *The Complete ArtScroll Siddur,* (New York 1984).

Jewish Prayer

The Need to Pray

The urge to express in words such deep emotions as fear, gratitude, confidence, happiness, pain, sorrow and love is an instinctive one. Words have the power to release pent-up emotions as well as to define them in rational and meaningful terms.

Where there exists a measure of conviction that our situation, happy or sad, is of concern to God, and that He can be moved to pity by human suffering, to anger by human ingratitude and to rejoicing by human appreciation, there also exists the urge to pray. Prayer is, therefore, not merely an aspect of religious ritual, but the expression of a religious impulse. The neglect of Prayer is inevitably the farewell salute to religion.

The Talmudic sages, by attributing to Abraham, Isaac and Jacob the introduction of the three statutory daily services, expressed in their own way this basic conception of Prayer as the natural libretto to the melody of Faith. When we speak, therefore, of the origins of Judaism we are referring at the same time to the dialogue between the Jew and his Maker through the medium of Prayer.

Spontaneity

Before the Talmudic period, the Temple and synagogue liturgy was characterised by a great deal of flexibility and spontaneity. It was only towards the end of the 1st century CE, due to the pioneering efforts of Rabban Gamliel II and his colleagues (see *Mishnah Berachot* 4:3-4) that a special order for the *Amidah* blessings, and an official text, or *nusach*, was made statutory.

It was because the Temple and its sacrificial order had been the primary focus of religious life for most of the pre-Common Era period that no need was felt to develop the liturgy and regulate the prayers. This frequently led to most unsatisfactory situations wherein people invited to lead the services at local prayer meetings became carried away with their own devotions, and burdened the congregation with long, drawn-out, extemporary prayers. Conversely, on other occasions, they became tongue-tied and lacked the spirit and facility to frame suitable blessings and praise of God.

Such a situation is reflected in an episode that occurred in the synagogue of Rabbi Eliezer's academy. On one occasion someone deputed to lead the service drew out the prayers for an interminable length of time. "How long-winded is this fellow!" the disciples complained to Rabbi Eliezer. "Is his prayer longer than that of Moses," replied the latter, "of whom it is stated: 'And I supplicated the Lord for forty days and forty nights' (Deuteronomy 9:25)?". On another occasion the one leading the service was unusually brief. When the disciples complained, Rabbi Eliezer replied, "Was his prayer any shorter than that of Moses who recited a mere five words (Numbers 12:13) when praying for his sister, Miriam, to be cured of her leprosy?" (*Talmud Berachot* 34a).

With the destruction of the Temple (70 CE), the *Bet Knesset* (synagogue) and the *Bet ha-Midrash* (Talmudic academy) took over its role as the main focus of religious and communal life. Both of these institutions co-operated in the development of Prayer, ensuring that it was not construed as but a pale substitute for the Temple sacrifices which were now suspended, but rather as a most up-lifting and edifying means of effecting a dialogue between the Jew and his Maker. The *Batei Midrash*, centres of study and keen debate between the Talmudists, who applied, developed and codified the accumulated legal and religious traditions of our people, made a particular contribution in the field of liturgy. Their members composed many spontaneous prayers and Blessings, as well as private meditations which they were accustomed to recite after their daily morning prayers. Many of the latter were preserved by their disciples and eventually formed an important part of our daily *Siddur* and Holyday *Machzor*.

Since the institution of the synagogue prided itself on being the successor of the Temple, a very real spiritual and emotional link was forged between the daily prayers of the synagogue and the daily sacrifices that had been offered in Temple times. Jewish national pride was thereby boosted by the synagogue, even though the Temple and Jerusalem lay in ruins. Through Prayer, the Jews reactivated the potent spiritual experience of the proximity to God felt in days gone by when participating in, or witnessing, the Temple ritual.

To give expression to such sentiments, rabbinic laws and discussions (*Mishnah*, *Beraita* and *Talmud*) pertaining to the sacrificial order came to be recited as part of the daily service. In a mystical sense, it was felt that God would accept the prayerful recollection of details of those sacrifices as if the latter were still being offered, and that divine grace and forgiveness would accordingly be directed towards the individual petitioner and, collectively, to the nation of Israel. Henceforth, study, in general, and of sacrificial law in particular, became elevated to an act of worship.

The Appeal of the Siddur

The appeal of the *Siddur* has never waned. It is among the precious constants in the life of the Jew. Notwithstanding the length of one's estrangement from it, it has the power to reactivate the religious impulse immediately. Just to take hold of it is to feel conditioned for Prayer. Just to open it up is to feel capable of extending oneself spiritually, of shedding one's preoccupation with the superficialities of life and of homing in on sacred and timeless concerns. Just to utter its familiar words and to chant its traditional melodies is to rediscover one's roots and the pure faith of one's childhood. It is to feel oneself standing on *terra firma*, buoyed up by a historic value system that does not capitulate to transient fashion or passing cultural whim.

The simple beauty of its language is breathtaking, and the unabashed directness of its appeal to the great Creator of the Universe to give ear to the simplest petition of His most lowly subjects is charmingly refreshing, while amazingly audacious. The *Siddur* gives us a confidence not only to address our Maker, but also to request that He address our concerns.

The effect of the *Siddur's* magic is felt long after it is put down. It spiritualizes not only the time it is in our hands, but also the rest of the day spent under its influence. It keeps the channels of communication open, acting also as a pressure valve for those who feel let down by fate, to challenge its justice.

The *Siddur* is often a treasured and nostalgic heirloom. What thoughts and emotions are stirred in the breasts of those fondly handling a prayer book purchased for their departed father's *Barmitzvah* by his father before him, and bearing an inscription redolent with love, blessing,

3

exhortation and expectation? What secret yearnings was that *Siddur* privy to? What hopes and fears for loved ones? What tears dropped silently on its pages? What glorious family gatherings on Sabbaths, festivals and special celebrations did it witness and consecrate? Such a *Siddur* binds the ages together in unity and faith. It affirms that this family is still constant to its Jewish values and traditions, and that the beacon handed down by its forebears is still burning brightly, revealing the way forward to its future progeny. More than any other book, the *Siddur* testifies to *Am Yisrael chay*, the life and vitality of the people of Israel; and, when it adorns a home, to the religious orientation of that family. It assuredly confirms the maxim that 'the family that prays together, stays together'.

In recent years, many Jewish schools and Hebrew classes have introduced the charming *Chagigat ha-Siddur* ('Celebration of the Prayer Book') ceremony, to mark the transition to the *Siddur* of the infant class that has just mastered Hebrew reading. This is considered a special landmark in the lives of the young people, and the *Chagigah* has taken its place almost as a new rite of passage.

A popular way of celebration is for the children to be called in turn to occupy the stage together with their parents, and for the latter to present their child with his or her *Siddur*, planting a kiss on their cheeks before returning to their seats. Many young parents have reported this to have been a most moving experience, and an incentive and challenge to re-think their own relationship to Prayer and the synagogue. They have subsequently enrolled in their synagogue's Hebrew Reading programme, ensuring a return to synagogue and to Jewish practice on the part of many who had hitherto stayed away out of embarrassment at their inability to read.

The Synagogue

The synagogue has been at the epicentre of Jewish life for over two thousand years. Some scholars attribute its origin to the Babylonian exile (586-537 BCE), where the Jews would have congregated for mutual support and nostalgic recollection, and where, at the same time, they would have offered prayers for their speedy restoration. It is suggested that those early periodic prayer-meetings gradually evolved into regular daily worship. This was not phased out on their return to Israel and the resumption of the sacrificial cult at the re-built Temple, but rather it continued and developed, and served especially those who lived too far away to visit the Temple. Other scholars place the origin of the synagogue much later, and account for it in other ways (See Jeffrey M. Cohen, *Blessed Are You*, N.J., Jason Aronson, Inc., pages 15-26).

The size and style of synagogue buildings varied from country to country, and period to period. They were generally a mirror of the general architecture of the day, allowing for certain restrictions that were frequently imposed on Jewish communities. Thus, while Jewish law recommends that the synagogue should be built on the highest site of a town, yet there was little chance of the Christian or Muslim authorities ever permitting this, especially as, traditionally, the church, with its spire reaching into the skies, sought the identical privilege, as did the Muslims with their lofty minarets.

In an Orthodox synagogue, a separation is made between the men's and women's section, in order to avoid distraction, communication or levity during Prayer. In the traditional, purpose-built synagogues, the women are accommodated in a special gallery. Where there is only one level, a *mechitzah* (divider) is provided. The height of this divider is frequently a cause of friction between the men and those women whose view of the proceedings might well be obscured, as well as between those men who view it as a mere symbolic separation, and others who believe - rightly or wrongly - that, indeed, it fulfils its purpose only if it obscures the women from the sight of the men!

The synagogue is perceived as a Temple-in-miniature. This means that the same reverence that was accorded the ancient Temple has to be accorded to the synagogue, that the structure and times of the three daily services are patterned on those of the Temple, that recollections and laws of the ancient sacrificial system are lovingly incorporated into many of the prayers, and that the focal point of the synagogue, the Ark, should face the east, the direction of Jerusalem and the Temple mount.

In this way, among others, Jews remained connected, over two thousand years of exile, to their spiritual source, and preserved within them the passionate longing to return to Zion, the abode of their God. Thus, synagogue Prayer constituted the most potent unifying force for Jewish nationalism and the preservation of the collective dynamic spirit of the Jewish people.

Decorum in Synagogue

Some authorities assert that maintaining the sanctity of the synagogue is a Biblical prescription, falling within the parameter of the verse, "And ye shall revere My sanctuary" (Leviticus 19:30). It is clearly of paramount importance, therefore, that the sanctity of the synagogue should not be compromised by improper or rowdy behaviour, immodest dress, levity, talking during the services or bringing very young children who are likely to distract or disturb other worshippers. The *Shulchan Aruch* prohibits having a chat with one's friend in a synagogue even when no service is in progress (*Orach Chayyim* 161:1)!

The great authority, Maimonides, was greatly troubled by the spectacle of those who were able to recite the silent *Amidah* for themselves chatting idly afterwards during its repetition while those who were not so knowledgeable were following it, word-for-word, together with the *Chazan*. He therefore took the extreme measure of actually abandoning the age-old tradition of reciting the silent *Amidah*, insisting that all had to recite together just one *Amidah* led by the *Chazan*. This practice remained in vogue in the communities which followed his guidelines for a period of some three hundred years.

Though it is recognised that occasionally an emergency arises, and it is necessary to speak or reply to one's neighbour or to the Wardens, care should be taken, however, to avoid interrupting one's prayers for the duration of the *P'sukei d'Zimra* (Morning Psalms). These all constitute one *mitzvah*-unit, introduced by the blessing *Baruch She-amar* (page 37 [58]) and concluding with the blessing *Yishtabach* (page 57 [82]); and one should obviously not interrupt in the middle of performing a unified *mitzvah*. For the same reason one may not talk from *Bor'chu* (page 59 [84]) until the end of the *Amidah* (page 89 [118]). *Bor'chu* introduces the blessings before the *Shema*; and the concluding blessing over the *Shema* - *Ga-al Yisra-el* (page 73 [96]) - must be linked to the *Amidah*. (Hence the *Chazan* recites the final two words, *Ga-al Yisra-el*, in an undertone, to prevent the congregation breaking that link with the *Amidah* by reciting *Amen* to his blessing). Thus, the blessings over the *Shema*, the *Shema* itself, its concluding blessings and the *Amidah* are construed as one long prayer, during the entirety of which one must not speak.

It is obviously strictly prohibited to talk while the *Torah* is being read, although between call-ups the regulation may be relaxed.

During certain parts of the service, even the responses of *Amen* and *Baruch hu uvaruch shemo* to the blessings of the *Chazan* (see below, page 20) are classified as interruptions and should not, therefore, be recited. This applies especially during one's recitation of the silent *Amidah*. If one lags behind, and is still reciting the silent *Amidah* when the *Chazan* has commenced his repetition, one does not interrupt to respond to his blessings, neither does one join in the congregational responses to the *Kedushah* or *Kaddish*. One merely pauses and listens silently to the *Chazan* and congregation and resumes thereafter one's silent *Amidah*. The regulations regarding the recitation of these responses at other points in the service are rather detailed, and beyond the scope of this digest.

The Minyan

Jewish Prayer is primarily congregational. That does not mean that we are not obligated to pray at home if we cannot get to synagogue to pray together with a congregation, but that, in the main, our prayers are couched in the plural. We pray *as* a community and *for* the community. This means that our own personal, self-centred petitions merge with, and are made secondary to, the needs and interests of *K'lal Yisra-el*, the Jewish national collective. This finds its clearest expression in the institution of the *minyan*, the quorum of ten adult Jewish males, perceived as a mini-community, that is required in order to hold a full congregational service, led by a *Chazan*, and engaging the congregation in a responsive interplay.

The precise number of ten males to constitute a *minyan* may be seen as derived from the episode of the twelve spies, of whom God said to Moses "How long shall I bear this evil *congregation*?" (Numbers 14:27). Now, two of the spies - Joshua and Caleb - were righteous; so God was applying the term 'congregation' to ten adult males. Hence the paradigm for the concept of the *minyan*, or mini-community.

Where a synagogue cannot muster ten males over the age of *Barmitzvah*, thirteen years, then those present simply pray silently, as individual worshippers. In that situation there can be no Reading of the *Torah*, no *Kaddish* (either Reader's or Mourner's), no responsive *Bor'chu*, and no repetition of the *Amidah*.

A common sight, around the time scheduled for the beginning of a service, is that of the Warden, or other individuals present, counting the people to see if the required ten males are present. Since Jewish tradition frowns on counting heads, like one counts sheep, it is customary to recite a particular verse, containing ten words, allocating a succeeding word to each person present. If the entire verse is allocated, then it is clear that there is a *minyan.* By the same token, it is easy to determine how many are still required to make up the quorum, on the basis of the words of the verse as yet unaccounted for.

The verse universally used is: *Hoshi-a et amecha uvarech et nachalatecha, ur'eim venas'eim ad ha-olam* - 'Save Thy people and bless Thine inheritance, tend them and carry them forever' (Psalm 28:9).

Swaying during Prayer

A Gentile visiting a synagogue for the first time will be struck by the curious sight of most of the worshippers swaying to and fro (Yiddish - *Shokling*) while praying. Although some authorities recommended a more dignified stance, believing that one should remain motionless and upright 'as a servant in the presence of his master', yet the custom of swaying rhythmically as an aid and stimulus to fervent concentration was universally preferred. To the western mind this expression of emotions during worship is considered somewhat undignified, notwithstanding the fact that, while dancing, any physical exuberance and uninhibited bodily gyrations are nowadays regarded as natural. Primitive dancing was, of course, an expression of religious emotion.

In Biblical times it was not uncommon for people to throw themselves prostrate to the ground, shout aloud or raise their hands above their head during Prayer. When the psalmist wrote "All my bones shall cry out: Lord, who is like Thee?" (Psalm 35:10), he was expressing the belief that not only the mouth, but the whole body should be involved in the act of worship.

II

The Synagogue Officials, Appurtenances and Responses

The Rabbi

'Rabbi' is a title that goes back some 2,000 years, to the sages who crystallized and formulated Jewish law and tradition, and whose debates and decisions formed the basis of the Talmudic literature. The term means, 'teacher', and those who have been awarded that title, throughout the ages, have always viewed that as their primary vocation.

A Rabbi is not a 'holy man'. High standards of moral conduct and a detectable measure of spirituality may be expected of him, but he has no obligations in that direction that are not incumbent upon any other committed Jew. The distinction of his title means no more than that he has mastered Talmudic literature and has been considered fit by illustrious Rabbinic academicians to receive *'semichah'* (ordination). This empowers him to offer guidance and render decisions in any areas of Jewish law and practice, and establishes his trustworthiness as a mentor and spiritual counsellor.

The course for the Rabbinate is pursued at a *Yeshivah*, a Rabbinical seminary, though few of these seminaries are geared exclusively to the training of Rabbis. A period of full-time study at a *Yeshivah* is regarded as an essential character-forming exercise and religious preparation for every Orthodox Jew who is intent upon living in accordance with the requirements of Jewish law. The Orthodox Jew must find some time each day for study of his heritage; and the central source of Judaism, the *Talmud*, requires several years of full-time study at a *Yeshivah* in order to be able to master its method, and to comprehend the later law codes and commentaries based upon it. The *Talmud* is written mainly in the Aramaic language, and the student is required to sit at the feet of master teachers in order to be initiated into its complex logical principles, style and methodology.

Most students devote one or two years to *Yeshivah* study before pursuing a trade or a university course. Some stay longer, and complete the entire programme of approximately five years. It is from the latter group of advanced students that the future Rabbis will be drawn. Having mastered the ability to study Rabbinic sources for themselves, and to make decisions based upon mature evaluation of those sources, a special course of study of practical *Halachah* (Jewish law) will be offered to them, on completion of which they will be awarded their *semichah*, and with it the title of 'Rabbi'. They are then, technically, ready to offer themselves to any community as its religious leaders. In practice, however, many graduates of *Yeshivot* realise that, if they are to win the respect and confidence of educated and professional people in their communities, they will be required to obtain a university degree. In Britain, Jews' College, and in America, the Yeshivah University, offer, in tandem, both a *Yeshivah* programme and academic courses in such subjects as Biblical studies, Jewish history, philosophy, mysticism, Hebrew language and literature, and Semitic languages.

But the picture is not yet complete. To cope with the multi-faceted problems of the modern world, with its high incidence of intermarriage, divorce, single-parentage, unemployment, drugs dependency, as well as a whole panoply of complex moral issues in the realm of medical and business ethics and personal relationships, the Rabbi has to possess a degree of worldliness and employ a whole range of skills that were hitherto undreamed-of in his profession. For this reason, great emphasis is now being placed upon the provision of in-service training for Rabbis.

There are many who believe, therefore, that too much is expected of the modern-day Rabbi. He has to be a traditional *Talmid chacham* (master of Talmudic literature), a scholar in the broadest sense, with the ability to relate Judaism to every modern-day scientific and ethical issue, an inspiring preacher, a witty after-dinner speaker, an educationalist, a counsellor, a communal organiser and fund-raiser, and a high-profile public figure. In many, smaller synagogues, the Rabbi is also expected to lead the services, to read the weekly portion of the Law and to teach in the Hebrew classes. In short, he is expected to be a 'Jack-of-all-synagogue-trades', which will inevitably leave him insufficient time to become a true master of any single one. (For a full survey of the historical and contemporary role of the Rabbi, see Jeffrey M. Cohen, *Blessed Are You,* pages 211-237.)

The Chazan

The term *Chazan* is borrowed from the context of the ancient Temple in Jerusalem, where one of the administrators bore the title, *Chazan ha-Knesset*, 'Overseer of the Congregation'. With the destruction of the Temple by the Romans, in the year 70 CE, a new emphasis was placed on Prayer and religious poetry, and many of the great Talmudic sages of the first few centuries CE turned their hands to the composition of blessings and prayers and the development of a basic liturgy. But they did not forget the Temple, which served as a formative influence, inspiration and the model upon which to pattern many aspects of the emerging institution of the synagogue and the regulations governing the laws of Prayer. Hence, the synagogue prayer leader subsequently became known by the term *Chazan*, evocative of Temple times.

The *Mishnah* (*Ta-anit* 2:1) already lays down guidelines for the type of man worthy to discharge the office of *Chazan*: He must be mature and conversant with the prayers as well as a father of children who struggles for his livelihood, so that he will pray with special urgency.

The *Talmud* (*Ta-anit* 16a) expands upon these qualities:

> He should be a well-adjusted individual who has an unassuming demeanour and is popular among people. He should be able to chant competently, and have a sweet voice. He should have a mastery of the Reading of the *Torah*, the Prophets and the Sacred Writings and should be conversant with *Midrash* and *Halachot* (Biblical exposition and religious law), and know every single blessing.

The role of *Chazan* was regarded as so important that the *Halachah* unashamedly states that 'in a community which needs to appoint both a Rabbi and a *Chazan*, but cannot afford both, the appointment of a *Chazan* takes priority, unless the Rabbi happens to be a most illustrious *Torah* personality who has a mastery of halachic decision-making' (*Shulchan Aruch, Orach Chayyim* 53: 24).

The late nineteenth century ushered in an era of unprecedented popularity for *Chazanim* and their art, which they enjoyed at least until the Second World War. This was the era of the great waves of immigration into the United States and Britain from Eastern Europe; and the immigrants brought their love of *Chazanut* to those shores. Large financial inducements were offered to the great *Chazanim* of the day to accept positions in the larger congregations and to make guest appearances, either at synagogue or on the concert platform. With the age of sound recordings, international reputations were gained for those 'artists', and the names of such *Chazanim* as Moishe Koussevitzky, Yossele Rosenblatt, Gershon Sirota, Berele Chagy, Leibele Glanz, Pinchas Pinchik and Mordechai Herschman, became legendary.

Alas, the golden age of *Chazanut* is now well past, especially for Orthodox congregations. Tastes have changed, and the vogue is for shorter, less formal services. Few synagogues can now afford to pay for the services of a Jewish Pavarotti; and, in any case, the average synagogue-goer now seeks his or her vocal entertainment on television or from compact discs, tapes and concerts. While a visit from the few contemporary 'greats' might pack a concert or synagogue hall, the appointment of a mega-*Chazan* is the exclusive privilege of just a handful of showpiece congregations in Israel and the USA.

In Britain, the demise of the full-time professional *Chazan* is almost complete, and there are no longer any training facilities for full-time *Chazanim*. The situation is such that, as an example, my own Stanmore and Canons Park Synagogue, with some 2,600 members, the largest membership of any Orthodox congregation in Europe, no longer employs a full-time *Chazan*! Interestingly, a number of the remaining *Chazanim* have changed course and studied for the Rabbinate, thereby offering their next communities the attractive package of a fully-qualified spiritual *factotum*.

Although changing tastes and economic factors have colluded to bring about this demise, it must certainly be lamented that a great tradition of liturgical music and a historic source of synagogal inspiration and spiritual beauty, must, in time, be lost forever.

The Shammash

Shammash means 'attendant, sexton'. To run effectively, every synagogue, in times past, employed a *Shammash*, whose tasks included opening up the synagogue early in the morning and locking it at night; overseeing its heating and lighting, its repairs and cleaning; setting-out and collecting-in the prayer books; ensuring that the *Torah* scrolls were rolled to the right place, in readiness for the following day's service, and that the correct cards (drawing attention to the special prayers to be inserted on special occasions and seasons) were slotted into the wall-display units.

Combined with his office was that of collector of membership dues, for which purpose he would make a special weekly visit to members' homes. When there were hardship cases (and when were there not?), he would also act as special charity collector. In the *shtetls* of Eastern Europe, he was also expected to be the *shulklapper*, getting up at an unearthly hour to knock on the front door of each home in order to rouse the men for Prayer. This was especially important during the High Holyday season, to awaken people before dawn to attend the *Selichot* (penitential) prayers.

During the services, his task was to ensure decorum. In many instances, the authority of his office in the eyes of the youngsters was such that one disapproving glance from him was sufficient to silence their chatter!

Wardens would come into office for a few years, and then leave, but the *Shammash* went on forever. He was an indispensable adviser to the Wardens, filling them in on the background to members, their families, their guests, their domestic situation, their celebrations and *yahrzeits*, and reminding them of who required to be called up to the *Torah*. He was frequently the first to detect that a family had fallen on hard times, and he would pass a discreet word to that effect to the organiser of the *Gemilut Chasadim* (welfare) society.

The *Shammash* was also the custodian of local *minhag* (tradition), and, as such, an indispensable guide to any new Rabbi. He also served as *Shadchan* (marriage broker) and co-ordinator of the *Chevra Kadisha* (Burial Society), and he would make all the synagogue and communal announcements at the end of the services. In essence, he was a veritable Communal Director.

The profession is now all but defunct, a casualty of economic constraints, changed social conditions and the age of computerization. Many of his valuable tasks have gone by default; others have been taken over by volunteer members who, by and large, do a competent job, but whose diplomacy cannot always be taken for granted. *Chaval al de'avdin vela mishtakchin* - "Alas, for that which is gone, but not forgotten!"

The Synagogue Officials, Appurtenances and Responses

SYNAGOGUE APPURTENANCES

The Ark

The focal point of the synagogue is the *Aron Kodesh*, the Sacred Ark, which houses the *Torah* Scrolls. Jewish law prescribes that the Ark be situated against the eastern wall, and congregants face the Ark to recite the central prayer, the *Amidah*.

The easterly direction symbolises the yearning for Jerusalem which burns deeply in the heart of Jewry and which constitutes a recurring theme in the liturgy. That this practice goes back to the earliest days of regularised worship may be inferred from the Biblical reference to Daniel (ca 540 BCE), who, though living in Babylon, 'had windows made in his roof-chamber looking towards Jerusalem' (Daniel 6: 10).

In large synagogues, the Ark is recessed into the wall, and the surrounding area is furnished with a decorative façade of symbolic design, usually embodying two Tablets of Stone bearing the initial words of each of the Ten Commandments. It is also customary to inscribe a Hebrew exhortation over the Ark, a popular choice being דַּע לִפְנֵי מִי אַתָּה עוֹמֵד ('Know before whom thou standest'). In synagogues which are not purpose-built, the Ark is often little more than a large cabinet with the Scrolls displayed in the upper section.

The Sefer Torah

The *Sefer Torah*, the Scroll of the Law, contains the Pentateuch or Five Books of Moses, a compound of history, law, symbolic ritual and moral guidance, commencing with the Creation and tracing the development of the Hebrew nation from Abraham through to the slavery in Egypt, the giving of the *Torah* at Mount Sinai and the forty years of wandering in the desert until the Israelites commenced their conquest of the Holy Land.

Although passages from the other two main sections of the Hebrew Bible - the Prophets and the Sacred Writings - also provide texts for synagogue reading, they do not compare in importance or sanctity with the Pentateuch. It is in the words of the Pentateuch that the Divine Revelation is described and the Divine Will communicated. It is from there that the spirit of Jewish nationalism draws its authentication, inspiration and impetus, and it is in that source that Israel's mission, law and religious ideology is delineated.

The unique sanctity of the Pentateuch is also expressed by the reverence accorded to the hand-written *Torah* Scrolls and the meticulous and detailed regulations that govern their preparation and writing. These regulations were codified in a special tract of the Talmud written over 1,400 years ago and followed in every detail to the present day. The preparation of the parchment, as well as the writing, is done by pious, skilled and learned men, called *Soferim*, Scribes. It is an art that calls for dedication as well as immense powers of concentration. The *Torah* is written with a quill pen fashioned from goose or turkey feathers and an ink preparation containing gall nuts, copper sulphate crystals and gum arabic. The parchment is made from the skin of a *Kosher* animal. There are 79,976 words in the *Torah*, and it takes up to a year for a skilled *Sofer*, working about eight hours a day, to complete the writing of a Scroll.

The *Sefer Torah* is provided with a decorative mantle and, where a synagogue can afford it, traditional silver ornaments. These consist of decorative crowns to which small bells are attached, a breast plate, at the centre of which there is often a miniature Ark or twelve stones representing the twelve tribes of Israel, and a silver pointer, or *Yad*, with which the Reader points to each word as he intones the portion of the Law.

The Parochet

The Scrolls are not visible during the greater part of the services, for, suspended from the front of the Ark, is the *Parochet*, the Ark curtain. This is traditionally of blue or red velvet, upon which is woven some symbolic representation, such as the seven-branched candelabrum as used in Temple times, or two lions. The choice of the latter was probably inspired by Isaiah 29: 1 which applies the term *Ariel*, 'Lion of God', to Jerusalem. Since the Ark faced Jerusalem the lion was regarded as an appropriate symbol.

The Duchan

Some distance in front of the Ark, in Talmudic times, was a raised platform, or *Duchan*, upon which the Priests would stand to bless the congregation. Such a platform was rendered redundant when the custom became widespread to elevate the Ark by actually placing it upon such a platform, with steps leading up to it. This has remained the accepted practice up to the present day. The size of the platform varies with each synagogue; some are veritable stages upon which are located the pulpit and two Ministers' boxes.

The Ner Tamid

Suspended on a level with the top of the Ark hangs the *Ner Tamid*, ('perpetual lamp'). This is to commemorate the candelabrum that was kept perpetually burning in the Jerusalem Temple, in accordance with Biblical Law. Although that light was replenished daily with pure olive oil, the modern *Ner Tamid* usually runs off electricity.

Mizrach

The fact that the Ark is in the centre of the eastern wall makes the seats in that area the most sought-after in the synagogue. Seats against the eastern wall, called *Mizrach*, are consequently reserved for synagogue and communal elders, scholars and men of distinction. Modern-day, large synagogues have dispensed with that arrangement, however, in the trend towards greater equality.

The Bimah

In the centre of the synagogue, facing towards the Ark, stands an oblong dais called the *Bimah* - 'high place'. At the front of it is the reading desk from which the *Chazan* leads the service and reads from the *Torah* Scrolls. The area in front of the *Bimah* and up to the Ark is traditionally left free of seating, and congregants do not cross over in front of the *Bimah*, even when participating in the service. An exception is made, however, in the case of the Wardens' box. These lay-leaders of the congregation are permitted to occupy an honoured position in front of the *Bimah*, facing the Ark. As the *Bimah* behind them is well raised up, they do not obscure the *Chazan*'s view of the Ark. Progressive synagogues have universally dispensed with the central *Bimah*. Their sevices are conducted from the front, with microphones ensuring full audibility.

The Ladies' Gallery

Another major difference between Orthodox and Reform synagogues lies in the place allocated to women worshippers. Orthodox practice has rigidly upheld the separation of the sexes during worship; and a characteristic of the Orthodox synagogue is its Ladies Gallery. For confirmation of their attitude, Orthodox authorities refer to the Temple of Jerusalem where the women occupied a special area, which also happened to be the most spacious of the Temple's courts.

The pioneers of Reform Judaism in the early 19th Century, who, in any case, were not in favour of linking synagogue practice to Temple tradition, swiftly abolished the segregation of women, and introduced family pews.

The Tallit - Prayer Shawl

The *Tallit*, worn by Jewish males during Prayer, is a four-cornered shawl of white wool, with blue or black stripes at the lower edge and a tassel of eight threads hanging from each corner. It was introduced in order to keep alive a Biblical ordinance requiring that the Jew be distinctive in his dress by attaching *Tzitzit* ('tassels') to the four corners of his garment. The Bible merely hints at the symbolic purpose of the tassels: 'And you shall look at them and remember all the commandments of the Lord and fulfill them' (Numbers 15: 39). The wearing of a sacred vestment throughout the day was to serve as an incentive to lead a moral, consecrated way of life.

Since the obligation of attaching *Tzitzit* came into force only when a garment actually had four corners, and since in the course of time such garments ceased to be worn, the Talmudic Rabbis instituted a special four-cornered garment, the *Tallit*, to be worn during Prayer in order to perpetuate the Biblically-prescribed wearing of *Tzitzit*. The name *Tallit* seems to have derived from the Aramaic word '*Istallit*' or '*Istola*', which is merely a variation of the Latin '*Stola*', the regular tunic worn in Roman times. Although we wear a *Tallit Katan* or *Tzitzit* under our garments, and recite a blessing over them, when we get to synagogue a further blessing is nevertheless required to be made over the larger *Tallit* since the intervening journey to synagogue constitutes an interruption, making the latter *mitzvah* into a separate ritual.

A woollen *Tallit* is preferable to other materials. It should be sufficiently large to cover most of the body, enabling one to lift it over the head and to sweep it over the left shoulder before reciting the blessing, 'Blessed art thou... who has commanded us to *enwrap* ourselves in the *Tzitzit*'.

If one removes one's *Tallit* temporarily, for example to attend to the needs of nature, intending to return as soon as possible and put it on again, one does not make another blessing on one's return. If, on the other hand, one removed it without such an intention, and then decided to return and put on the *Tallit*, a fresh blessing is required. It is also required when replacing a *Tallit* that has inadvertently fallen off completely. The *Tallit* is worn every day of the year (unlike *Tefillin* which are not worn on Sabbath and festivals). On the fast of *Tisha b'Av*, the *Tallit* and *Tefillin* are worn in the afternoon, to the *Minchah* service.

The Tefillin

These are leather boxes containing Biblical passages which are secured on the head and arm by means of straps, *Retsuot*, and which are worn on weekdays for the duration of the Morning Service. The obligation to wear *Tefillin* devolves upon males immediately they have attained their *Barmitzvah*.

Four times in the *Torah* we are commanded to bind upon ourselves specific passages from the Scriptures as a constant reminder of the unique relationship existing between Israel and God. The Bible does not limit the wearing of *Tefillin* to any particular time, but seems to demand that they be worn throughout the day.

During the first few centuries CE, the Romans prohibited the wearing of *Tefillin*, with the result that Jews contented themselves with putting them on in private, merely for the duration of their morning prayers. It was this restricted use of the *Tefillin* which later became the norm and which is responsible for the post-Biblical name, *Tefillin*, 'prayer accompaniments', being applied to them. The popular early translation of *Tefillin* by the word 'Phylactery' is incorrect. 'Phylactery' is a Greek word meaning 'a guard' or 'protector', and reflects the superstitious notion that they were meant to guard against disease and evil spirits. Some may have viewed them in this light, but Jewish tradition always regarded them as an outward sign of Israel's commitment to live by the Divine Law.

The hand-*Tefillin* is worn on the weaker arm, which is the left one, unless one is left-handed when they are worn on the right arm. The hand with which we write is taken as the criterion of strength. An ambidextrous person follows the majority and places it on his left arm. In the unusual situation of a right-handed person who, nevertheless, uses his left hand exclusively for writing, he would be required to wear his *Tefillin* on his right arm, as that is his 'weaker' hand in respect of writing.

One may not speak or even gesticulate while putting on the hand- and head-*Tefillin*. The same applies even for the sake of interrupting in order to make the congregational responses to the *Kaddish* or *Kedushah*. The only exception to this is if one hears one's neighbour reciting the blessings over the *Tefillin*. He may affirm this *mitzvah* by reciting *Amen*, as this is not regarded as an interruption of an extraneous theme, being the very *mitzvah* upon which he is currently engaged. (For more *Tefillin* regulations, see below, page 35).

The Covering of the Head

It is obligatory for Jews to cover their heads while they are in synagogue, when reciting any prayer or blessing at home or reading sacred literature. Orthodox Jews will not walk in the street or indulge in any type of leisure activity without a head-covering, and they are distinguishable by the variety of their skull-caps. Modern Orthodoxy favours the *kipah s'rugah*, (knitted skull-cap), while those to the right of the religious spectrum have a preference for the black velvet variety, the traditional '*yarmulkah*' (head covering). The shape and decoration of these is an art form in itself, reflecting the great variety of cultural backgrounds the Jewish people have come from. Some branches of Orthodox Jewry feel that the small *yarmulkah*-type of head-coverings are unsuitable, and choose to wear hats with a characteristic, wide brim.

The *Zohar* offers a mystical reason for covering the head, suggesting that since the *Shechinah* - 'Divine Spirit' - hovers above a person, the head should be covered as a mark of respect. A more realistic suggestion is offered by David Halevi of Ostrog (17th Century), namely that the practice was introduced as a reaction to the Christian mode of worshipping with head bared.

RESPONSES

Amen

The *Amen* response, as a token of affirmation, is found in the *Torah* (Numbers 5: 22; Deuteronomy 27: 15-26). In the book of Jeremiah we have the clearest expression of the sense in which the utterance *Amen* was employed: 'And Jeremiah the Prophet said: *Amen,* may God *confirm* the prophecy you have made to restore the vessels of the house of God and all the exile, from Babylon to this place'. (Jeremiah 28: 6). The respondent 'confirms' thereby that 'the blessing he has just heard recited is true and that he believes implicitly in it' (*Orach Chayyim* 124: 6).

We are required to concentrate carefully when reciting *Amen,* to ensure that the word is clearly and fully enunciated, and that this response is not commenced before the person has actually fully completed the last word of the blessing. This is dubbed an *Amen chatufah,* 'a snatched response'. Conversely, one should not delay unduly before reciting the *Amen* response. This is called an *Amen yetomah,* 'an orphaned response'. We do not recite *Amen* after our own blessings; the only exception to this rule is the blessing *Boneh verachamav Yerushalayim (Amen)* in the Grace after Meals. There the *Amen* marks off the earlier three blessings, which are accorded Biblical status, from the fourth which was added in the later Rabbinic period.

Baruch hu uvaruch shemo

The response *Baruch hu uvaruch shemo* is made when hearing the *Chazan* or another recite the Divine name in the context of a blessing. This response is omitted when one requires to fulfill one's own *mitzvah* by listening to the recitation of a blessing, as, for example, when listening to the blessings recited over the *Shofar,* the *Megillat Esther* or by one called up to the Reading of the Law. Similarly, one does not make the response on hearing the *Chazan* recite the blessings before and after the *Shema,* but they are recited as a response to his *Birkot ha-Shachar* (see page 37) and during the Repetition of the *Amidah.*

III

History and Efficacy of Jewish Prayer

In Talmudic times there was a dogged insistence that no oral traditions - and that included blessings and prayers - should be committed to writing. Nevertheless, by the 8th century, Yehudai Gaon (*Gaon*, 'excellency', was the title given to the spiritual leader and supreme halachic authority of Babylonian Jewry) already refers to the existence of unofficial prayer books. He does not authorise their general introduction, but he does permit the Reader to use a *Siddur*, written text, on occasions such as the Day of Atonement, when the service is prolonged by unfamiliar compositions.

During the succeeding century, written texts must have been smuggled into the synagogue, subsequently becoming an indispensable aid to prayer. Popular pressure for a standard prayer book prompted the Spanish community of Lucena to write to the Babylonian *Gaon*, Natronai (ca 860) on the subject. His response constituted the nucleus of a prayer book. Basing himself on the Talmudic tradition that a man is duty-bound to recite one hundred blessings each day, Natronai arranged his *Siddur* to conform to this pattern, listing in full the *Meah berachot*, one hundred obligatory blessings.

Natronai's successor as *Gaon* was Amram bar Sheshna. His *Seder Rav Amram* constitutes the first attempt to produce a systematic text of the prayers rather than a mere list of blessings; and this *Siddur* was quoted extensively by Rashi, Tosaphot, Karo and many later authorities. Amram included in his *Seder* an halachic section dealing with explanations of the liturgy and regulations governing Prayer, which greatly added to the esteem in which the work was held throughout France and Spain.

By far the greatest liturgical work of the Middle Ages was the *Siddur* of Saadia Gaon (892-942), one of the most illustrious of Jewish scholars. Accompanying the Hebrew text are regulations regarding Prayer and synagogal customs. The latter are written in Arabic and embody Saadia's criticisms of a number of existing prayers and compositions which either 'have no root in tradition' or which 'spoil the intention' of the prayer they come to supplement. Saadia travelled extensively, and his decision to compile an authorised prayer book was clearly prompted by 'the neglect, addition and omission' he witnessed in synagogues at home and abroad. His solution was to provide a prayer book which he hoped would further his ambition of unifying the Jewish world.

The great philosopher and halachist, Moses Maimonides (1135-1204) also compiled a prayer book, entitled *Seder Tefillot Kol Hashanah*, which is incorporated into his Code of Law, the *Mishneh Torah*. Maimonides strongly opposed any interruption in the standard service, even for the sake of reciting a private petition. He was, thus, against the recitation of *piyyutim*, the poetic supplements we recite on festivals.

One of Rashi's close disciples, Simcha ben Samuel (d. 1105), from the town of Vitri, in Northern France, compiled a prayer book, the *Machzor Vitri*, reflecting the existing rite. This was much the same rite as followed by the pre-expulsion Jews of England as well as by the Ashkenazi communities of South-West Germany.

Ashkenazi and Sephardi Rites

The liturgies of the Ashkenazi (Central and Eastern European) and Sephardi (Spanish and Portuguese) communities have always been characterised by differences. Why these differences existed was never satisfactorily explained until Leopold Zunz, who laid the groundwork for the study of the liturgy during the last century, propounded the theory that they are not merely due to the varying traditions of medieval Germany and Spain, but have their origin in the more ancient distinction between the liturgies of Palestine and Babylon.

The influence of the Babylonian rite dominated the Arab countries, especially Spain, which frequently sought the guidance of the Babylonian *Geonim*. The Palestinian ritual did not, as might be supposed, die out as Jewish life waned, from the 4th Century CE, but was transplanted to Christian Europe to become the basis of the Ashkenazi tradition.

From the 11th century, the Ashkenazi and Sephardi liturgies diverged further, as German Rabbis tried their hand, with varying degrees of success, at liturgical and poetic expression. The most notable contribution to the Ashkenazi ritual during this period was by the Kalonymos family, Kalonymos ben Meshullam, Moses Kalonymos and his sons Kalonymos and Yekutiel.

The Crusades left an indelible mark on the liturgy as memorial dirges and *Kinot* (laments) were composed to describe and bemoan the tragedy. The *Aleinu* prayer, especially dear to the martyrs, many of whom recited it as they breathed their last, was thus moved from its position in the *Rosh Hashanah* liturgy to a place of honour at the conclusion of every service.

The countries east of the Danube developed, in the course of time, their own variations of the Ashkenazi ritual. Differing traditions, with regard to the order of the prayers and the inclusion or exclusion of certain compositions and phrases, were responsible for the variations found in the Prayer rites of even the individual towns and provinces of these countries. It was the Polish rite that became dominant in England; and it is upon that rite that the *Singer's Prayer Book* is based.

The Efficacy of Prayer

A question that is frequently asked is, "What is Prayer?". This begs the supplementary question: "Can a little speck in the vast universe, truly address the Infinite?".

The answer is that Prayer is precisely what converts that little speck into an entity of inestimable and cosmic significance. Prayer is the signal we transmit into that vast universe, to engage the attention of the God who created it, and who can, and does, assuredly traverse it to enter into proximity and dialogue with man. It is only Prayer that has the power to convince man that he is more than an accident of Creation. To apply A J Heschel's phrase: If God is, indeed, 'in search of man', then Prayer is man's way of saying *hinneini*, "Here I am, Lord. Speak, for Your servant hears; and listen, for Your child loves and needs You".

As to people who just cannot warm to preformulated Prayer, but want, rather, to speak to God directly, they should certainly be encouraged to attempt to do so, but should be aware that not only is it not enough, but that it is also not as easy as it sounds, to address the Almighty God in terms that are religiously appropriate. Such people will probably end up in a state of inadequacy and embarrassment when it comes to enunciating their own individualistic praise of Him. They will probably resort to merely paraphrasing, rather poorly, existing forms and phraseology, which will, of course, defeat their avowed purpose! The likelihood is that their petitions and personal pleas will also be couched as unacceptable, self-centred, brusque and overly-demanding modes of expression, a mere out-pouring of their problems and complaints, with no sense of balance or proportion.

Their words will undoubtedly be heard, but they will certainly bear the imprint of their own selfish needs and desires. They will, of necessity, relate to God from the vantage-point of exclusivity, whereas the Jewish way is inclusive. We feel and pray with and for the community as a whole; for the less fortunate, for our homeland and for our national aspirations. Their extemporary words will be heard, but they will inevitably be unworthy containers for such lofty spiritual ingredients.

For the language of Prayer, we Jews have traditionally borrowed from the holy and inspired phraseology of our Bible, as well as from the unique liturgical vocabulary that generations of our Rabbinic luminaries have assured us is the most appropriate genre for such an intimate and sacred exercise. Those words are suffused with national and historical reminiscences. They are the perfectly-tuned instruments of Prayer, whereas the private extemporised words may well be discordant.

And even when the individual worshipper does feel able to muster appropriate forms of expression, how frequently can he be assured of being inspired and creative? And when the spirit and inspiration just does not come, will he or she simply refrain from praying? It is a habit one can easily get out of. My advice is to continue to recite the existing prayers, and to use them as spring-boards for one's own, personal emotional outpouring. Indeed, that is an acceptable, some might say ideal, form of *kavanah*, religious concentration.

IV

Women's Prayer Obligations

It is a fact that the obligation of women to pray is far more circumscribed than that of men. Although modern progressive thinking might regard such a view as anathema, Judaism recognized the home as being a co-partner with the synagogue in the nurturing of spirituality, and accorded the woman, as primary home-maker, the greatest consideration. Her domestic routine was regarded, therefore, as taking priority over the thrice-daily synagogue routine to which her husband was committed.

At the same time, the Rabbis recognised women's psychological and spiritual need to pray, in order to seek Divine mercy and guidance, and, in general, to have a conduit to express their inner fears, hopes, aspirations and gratitude. This need had to be accommodated, however, within the overarching principle governing women's religious obligations, namely that they are absolved from performing positive Biblical commandments or rituals that are confined to a specific time of the day or year.

According to this principle, it might be thought that women should be absolved entirely from daily Prayer which is, after all, regulated by time, in the form of morning, afternoon and evening services. The view of Maimonides was that, since women are absolved only from time-regulated Biblical rituals, and since, in Biblical times, Prayer was not prescribed for any particular time of the day - it being left to the individual when, and how frequently, he or she wished to pray - Prayer should not, therefore, be construed as 'time-related', and it consequently remains obligatory for women. Even though the later Rabbis introduced the thrice-daily recitation of the *Amidah* (which, technically, makes it 'time-related'), yet, for Maimonides, this does not absolve women, since the original flexibility of the Biblical institution of Prayer continues to determine its status as regards their obligations.

Although, according to that authority, women are obligated to pray on a daily basis - and by 'Prayer' we refer primarily to the *Amidah* composition, yet some later authorities differed as to precisely what form Maimonides required women's prayer to take. Some assumed that he

25

required them to recite all three daily *Amidahs*; others believed that they were required to recite only two, since the Evening Service originally had merely an optional status; while a third view has it that Maimonides' requirement is satisfied by the mere recitation of some brief, even self-composed, form of liturgical expression or petition.

The daily recitation of the *Shema* is clearly a positive 'time-related' Biblical prescription since it states that this mitzvah should be performed 'when you lie down and when you rise up' (Deuteronomy 6:7). Hence women are not obligated to recite it. Later authorities recommend at least the recitation of its opening line, containing the acceptance of the yoke of the kingdom of heaven. The *Aruch ha-Shulchan* commends not only the recitation of the *Shema* but also its two introductory blessings.

Magen Avraham regards the *G'ulah* (redemption) blessing, which follows the *Shema* and leads into the *Amidah,* as incumbent upon women. This is because the *Halachah* prescribes that it be joined to the *Amidah* without interruption (even for the recitation of *Amen*), for which reason it is recited by the Reader in an undertone. Hence, just as the *Amidah* is incumbent upon women, so also is the accompanying *G'ulah* blessing. Its obligatory nature may also be accounted for on the basis that women have an equal stake in the 'redemption' of Israel.

The latter consideration is also invoked to recommend that women include recitation of the entire concluding section of the Morning Service, namely *Ashrei, Lam'natze-ach, Uva l'tzion, Aleinu* and *Shir shel yom* (the daily psalm), which deal predominantly with the Messianic redemption.

Tachanun consists of prayers for mercy and forgiveness. Since, according to Nachmanides, that is the key purpose of Prayer, it follows that women should be given the opportunity to express these *Tachanun* sentiments. Other core sections of the daily service which women should recite include the early morning *Torah* and *Birkot ha-Shachar* blessings (see below, page 37). The recitation of the *Baruch She-amar*, the *P'sukei d'Zimra* (Morning Psalms), and *Yishtabach* remains optional.

The Afternoon Service (*Minchah*) is recited, according to the *Talmud*, at a time especially propitious for prayers to be answered; hence, according to some authorities, women have an obligation to recite that *Amidah*. The Evening Service (*Ma-ariv*), began as an optional service since it did not correspond to the offering of any sacrifice in Temple times. For this reason, all authorities agree that women are absolved from its recitation.

Although women are exempt from the obligation of reciting *Hallel* (a 'time-related' composition) and *Musaf* (the Additional Service), yet they have acccepted upon themselves their recitation as obligatory. Ashkenazi women may also recite the blessing over *Hallel*, even though they are not *'commanded* to recite the *Hallel'*. Sephardi women are not permitted by their authorities to recite such a blessing where no obligation exists.

Women's Tefillah Groups

Recent years have witnessed the establishment of a number of Women's *Tefillah* Groups, meeting the expressed need of informed and observant Orthodox women for their own public, yet intimate, act of worship. Such a setting provides them with the opportunity to be more spiritually active, demonstrative and uninhibited, and to frame a form of service that is more in focus with their own requirements (within the halachic parameters), and wherein they can encourage their fellow women to increase their levels of observance and Jewish knowledge.

The idea was born in New York, and introduced, with the blessing of Rabbi Shlomo Riskin, into his Lincoln Square Synagogue. It was taken up in Britain around 1987 by Orthodox students at Cambridge University who secured Chief Rabbi Immanuel Jakobovits' permission to hold such a service, subject to the clear halachic guidelines he provided.

The subject became something of a *cause célèbre* a few years later when the present writer gave permission for a local group to hold its services in his Stanmore and Canons Park Synagogue. After colleagues expressed strong feelings that this sort of innovation should not be encouraged, the Chief Rabbi, Dr Jonathan Sacks, issued revised guidelines, effectively permitting the services, though not on synagogue premises. The most successful group, the Stanmore Women's *Tefillah* Group, accordingly meets at a venue near the synagogue, and services are held approximately every six weeks. A number of girls have held their *Batmitzvah* ceremonies as part of the service, and have read their portion, with the traditional chant (*trope*), though from a *Chumash*, rather than a *Sefer Torah*.

On the subject of the use of a *Sefer Torah* by women, the vast majority of halachic authorities find no prohibition. Even contact with it during the period of menstruation is not forbidden, on the basis of the principle that 'words of *Torah* are not susceptible to uncleanliness'. *Torah* is a neutralizing agent. It purifies hearts, minds and bodies, and nothing can demean its pure status. Nevertheless, neither the former nor present Chief Rabbi has deemed it advisable to permit the use of a *Sefer Torah*, possibly out of fear that this might tempt the women to introduce the traditional seven *aliyyot* ('call-ups') and recite the responsive *Bor'chu* blessing, which may only be performed in the context of a male *minyan*.

This leads us to the principle of what is, and is not, permitted in the context of a Women's *Tefillah* Group. Essentially, women are more individualistic than men, and do not merge naturally into a *minyan*, a mini-community. Thus, those parts and elements of the prayers for which a *minyan* (ten males) is essential, and which involve the responsive interplay of Reader and congregation, may not be recited by women. This includes the recitation of *Bor'chu*, wherein the Reader summons the congregation (*minyan*) to 'Bless the Lord (*Bor'chu et Adonai...*) who is to be blessed', to which the congregation makes a dutiful response: *Baruch Adonai ham'vorach l'olam va'ed*. Hence women may not be called up to the *Torah*, since this involves the recitation of that identical responsive *Bor'chu* blessing.

The *Kaddish* is another prayer that requires a *minyan* of men. Again, the Reader addresses the congregation and directs them to "Say *Amen*" (*v'imru Amen*) - a characteristically responsive element of public worship which may not, therefore, form part of a women's service.

We have already observed that the repetition of the *Amidah* was originally prescribed in order to enable those who did not know their Hebrew prayers, to follow them with the *Chazan*, word for word. (At that time it was actually prohibited to commit the prayers to writing.) Again, since this repetition was an exercise in enabling the bulk of 'the congregation' to fulfil its duty of Prayer, its recitation was also prohibited for women, whose status remains that of private worshippers. Another consideration is that the repetition of the *Amidah* contains the *Kedushah*, which involves a responsive interplay between Reader and congregation.

Notwithstanding these restrictions, the Women's *Tefillah* groups have created a most inspirational form of service, supplemented by other meaningful traditional readings and *divrei Torah*, that make their services most enjoyable and spiritually uplifting for all participants.

V

Service for Weekday Mornings
תְּפִלַּת שַׁחֲרִית לַחוֹל

page 1
(*Singer's*)

page [12]
(*ArtScroll*)

The section commencing with וַאֲנִי בְּרֹב חַסְדְּךָ, until עֲנֵנִי בֶּאֱמֶת יִשְׁעֶךָ, is recited upon entering the synagogue. These verses describe the combination of joy and awe which should characterise our worship of God, and they call upon Him to grant the fulfilment of our petitions. The *ArtScroll Siddur* places the section on entering the synagogue *after* the putting on of *Tallit* and *Tefillin*, reflecting the common practice in a bygone age of donning these before leaving the home to walk to the Synagogue.

page 3 [4]

PUTTING ON THE *TALLIT*

The *Tallit* is taken out and draped over the shoulders, during which time the section הִנְנִי מִתְעַטֵּף בְּטַלִּית is recited. The *Tallit* is then lifted over the head, and swept over the left shoulder, and the following *b'rachah* is recited:

בָּרוּךְ אַתָּה יְיָ אֱלֹהֵינוּ מֶלֶךְ הָעוֹלָם,
אֲשֶׁר קִדְּשָׁנוּ בְּמִצְוֹתָיו וְצִוָּנוּ לְהִתְעַטֵּף בַּצִּיצִת.

PUTTING ON THE *TEFILLIN* IN EASY STAGES

page 5 [6]

The paragraph commencing הִנְנִי מְכַוֵּן בַּהֲנָחַת תְּפִילִין is a meditation to be recited while taking out and unwinding the hand-*Tefillin*.

First Stage

The left arm is slipped through the loop formed when the strap of the hand-*Tefillin* is unwound (see fig. 1, next page).

29

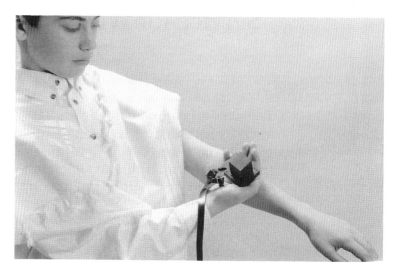

Fig. 1 - First Stage

Second Stage   The box is positioned so that it rests on the muscle of the left arm, or, in the case of a left-handed person, the right arm (see fig. 2, below).

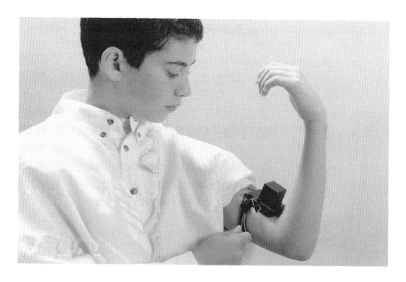

Fig. 2 - Second Stage

Third Stage.   After reciting the blessing

בָּרוּךְ אַתָּה יְיָ אֱלֹהֵינוּ מֶלֶךְ הָעוֹלָם,
אֲשֶׁר קִדְּשָׁנוּ בְּמִצְוֹתָיו וְצִוָּנוּ לְהָנִיחַ תְּפִלִּין.

the strap is tightened, with the box inclining towards the heart.

The strap is then wound over the forearm seven times (see fig. 3, below).

Fig. 3 - Third Stage

Fourth Stage   The head-*Tefillin* is then taken out and unwound. The shape for the head is made by opening out the straps between the fingers of both hands (see fig. 4, next page).

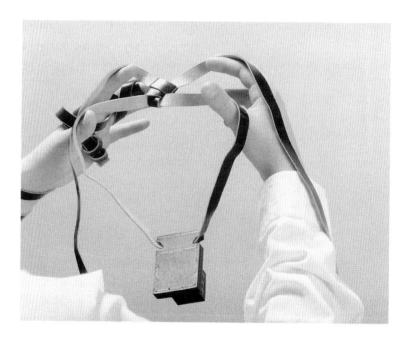

Fig. 4 - Fourth Stage

Fifth Stage

It is then lifted over on to the head with the box resting loosely at the front hairline. (See fig. 5a, next page).

The following blessing is then recited:

בָּרוּךְ אַתָּה יְיָ אֱלֹהֵינוּ מֶלֶךְ הָעוֹלָם,
אֲשֶׁר קִדְּשָׁנוּ בְּמִצְוֹתָיו וְצִוָּנוּ עַל מִצְוַת תְּפִלִּין.

It is then tightened firmly on the head so that the horizontal base of the head-*Tefillin* meets the hair line at the forehead.

In the correct position the knot at the back should rest against the nape of the neck (see fig. 5b, next page).

When one is satisfied that the head-*Tefillin* is securely and correctly positioned, the following line is recited:

בָּרוּךְ שֵׁם כְּבוֹד מַלְכוּתוֹ לְעוֹלָם וָעֶד

32

Fig. 5a   *Fifth Stage*   *Fig. 5b*

Sixth Stage   The strap of the hand-*Tefillin* is wound three times over the middle finger (see fig. 6a, below): once over

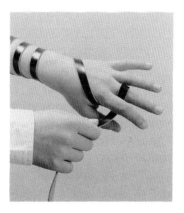 

Fig. 6a   *Sixth Stage*   *Fig. 6b*

33

the bottom section of the finger, then over the upper section of the finger, and finally brought back again on top of the lower section (see fig. 6b, previous page).

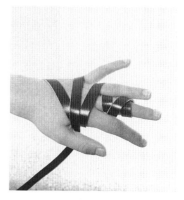

Fig. 6c   *Sixth Stage*   *Fig. 6d*

It is then looped over the ring finger (see fig. 6c, above); and then wound over the top of the hand so as to depict the Hebrew letter *Shin*, שׁ, denoting *Shaddai*, the Divine name (see fig. 6d, above).

page 7 [8]

While winding the strap over the middle finger and the top of the hand, one recites the middle paragraph:

וְאֵרַשְׂתִּיךְ לִי לְעוֹלָם,
וְאֵרַשְׂתִּיךְ לִי בְּצֶדֶק,
וּבְמִשְׁפָּט וּבְחֶסֶד וּבְרַחֲמִים.
וְאֵרַשְׂתִּיךְ לִי בֶּאֱמוּנָה,
וְיָדַעַתְּ אֶת יְיָ.

Seventh Stage

Finally, that section of the strap of the hand-*Tefillin* still remaining over is wound around the middle of the hand, as many times as necessary, so as to maintain the shape of the letter *Shin* (see fig. 7, next page).

34

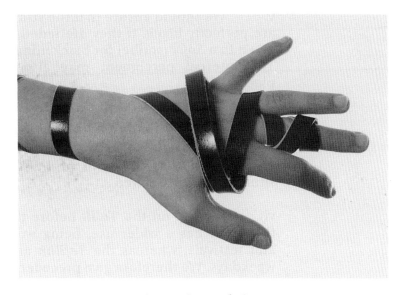

Fig. 7 - Seventh Stage

TEFILLIN FACTS

i.   We stand while putting on, and taking off, the *Tefillin*.

ii.   We must not talk or interrupt during the entire time that we are engaged on putting on both the hand- and the head-*Tefillin*.

iii.   Since the *Tefillin* contain parchments on which passages from the *Torah* are written, it follows that the whole time they are on our body we should behave in a decorous and respectful way, as if we were holding a *Sefer Torah* in our arms.

iv.   If we are in the middle of putting on the *Tefillin* when the Reader is reciting the Morning Blessings, we do not respond with *Baruch hu uvaruch shemo* and *Amen*, in the usual way. We just stop putting on the *Tefillin* and listen to the blessings until they are completed. We then resume binding on the *Tefillin*.

v.   We should ensure that the straps of the *Tefillin* are perfectly black. If they are faded, they should be taken to a *Sofer* (scribe) for blackening and examining. The internal parchment may also have faded in places.

vi.   Just as in the case of a *Sefer Torah*, if a single letter, or part of a letter, of the script is missing, worn away, perforated or illegible, it may not be used, so also the *Tefillin* are *pasul* (unfit for use), in that situation, until repaired.

vii.   We put on the *Tallit* before the *Tefillin* since the *Tallit* has a wider use, being worn on Sabbaths and festivals, whereas the *Tefillin* are worn only on weekdays. We therefore give precedence to the *Tallit*.

viii.   If, however, one took one's *Tefillin* out of the bag before the *Tallit*, then one should put on the *Tefillin* first, because of the principle, *Ein ma-avirin al ha-mitzvot*, 'We do not by-pass mitzvot'.

ix.   There is, however, one exception to that principle, however, and that is if he inadvertently took out the head-*Tefillin* first. We then set aside that Rabbinic principle, since the *Torah* itself accords precedence to the hand-*Tefillin*, when it states, 'And it shall be for a sign upon your hand, and as frontlets before your eyes'. In such a situation, he should put the head-*Tefillin* down on the desk and cover it with his *Tallit* bag before proceeding to put on the hand-*Tefillin*.

x.   If one mislaid one's *Tefillin*, one may still pray the Morning Service without them (for fear that the prescribed time before which *Shema* and the *Amidah* should be recited might pass), and later in the day - when one has located them or borrowed a pair - one may still put them on, as long as it is still day. In such a situation, one should recite a psalm or pray the Afternoon Service with them on.

THE SERVICE COMMENCES

page 9 [12]   The אֲדוֹן עוֹלָם is not recited aloud by the Reader or prescribed as part of the congregational service.

page 11 [12]   The familiar hymn יִגְדַּל is similarly only for silent meditation, if time permits, as a prelude to the service. It is a poetic representation of Maimonides' 'Thirteen Principles of the Jewish Faith', which appears on page 153 of *Singer's* and page 178 of *ArtScroll*.

page 13 [14]   The *Birkot ha-Shachar* ('Morning Blessings'), on this page, are recited silently. For the Jew, cleanliness is next to godliness. The first blessing (עַל נְטִילַת יָדָיִם) is consequently one for washing of hands, which is obligatory on awakening from sleep. The second blessing, אֲשֶׁר יָצַר, is prescribed for recitation after attending to nature's needs. It refers to the complexity of the human body and the gift of good health. The next three blessings refer to the most precious gift in Israel's possession, that of the *Torah*.

After the above *Torah* blessings, it is logical to quote a verse from the *Torah*. The choice is the Biblical formula for the Priestly Blessing as recited daily in Temple times:

יְבָרֶכְךָ יְיָ וְיִשְׁמְרֶךָ.
יָאֵר יְיָ פָּנָיו אֵלֶיךָ וִיחֻנֶּךָּ.
יִשָּׂא יְיָ פָּנָיו אֵלֶיךָ וְיָשֵׂם לְךָ שָׁלוֹם.

page 13 [16]   The next section, commencing with the words

אֵלּוּ דְבָרִים שֶׁאֵין לָהֶם שִׁעוּר

is from the *Mishnah*, Israel's Oral Law, which, together with the written *Torah*, enjoys an equally binding, inseparable authority. The concluding phrase of this Mishnah, וְתַלְמוּד תּוֹרָה כְּנֶגֶד כֻּלָּם, 'and (the reward for) study of the *Torah* exceeds them all', made it a most suitable passage for recitation in the context of *Torah* benedictions.

page 15 [18] The last of the silent prayers, אֱלֹהַי נְשָׁמָה, is recited by way of introduction to the congregational Morning Service. As these prayers are recited soon after waking from one's sleep, the poetic reference to the soul returning to the body is appropriate.

The Reader commences the service by reading aloud all but the last (הַמַּעֲבִיר שֵׁנָה) of the fifteen blessings on this and the following page, commencing:

בָּרוּךְ אַתָּה יְיָ . . . לְהַבְחִין בֵּין יוֹם וּבֵין לָיְלָה:

and ending with the blessing:

בָּרוּךְ אַתָּה יְיָ . . . הַנּוֹתֵן לַיָּעֵף כֹּחַ.

The congregation answers בָּרוּךְ הוּא וּבָרוּךְ שְׁמוֹ after the third word (the name of God) in each blessing, and אָמֵן at the end.

page 17 [20] The Reader recites from וּתְנֵנוּ הַיּוֹם until the end of the blessing גּוֹמֵל חֲסָדִים טוֹבִים לְעַמּוֹ יִשְׂרָאֵל, after which the congregation recites silently the next few paragraphs. Few congregations recite *ArtScroll's* pages 22-24 (inclusive).

page 19 [26] The Reader recites aloud the last two lines of the לְפִיכָךְ section, and, after the words פַּעֲמַיִם בְּכָל יוֹם, the congregation recites in a loud voice the line

שְׁמַע יִשְׂרָאֵל, יְיָ אֱלֹהֵינוּ, יְיָ אֶחָד.

page 21 [28] The Reader concludes by reciting aloud the last two lines before the blessing:

בָּרוּךְ אַתָּה יְיָ מְקַדֵּשׁ אֶת שִׁמְךָ בָּרַבִּים.

In most congregations the next few pages, dealing with details of the daily offerings in the Temple, as

38

recorded in the Bible and in Rabbinic literature, are recited silently and fairly rapidly. *ArtScroll's* additional passages, on pages 30 to 32 (middle), and 34 to 42, are not said in most congregations.

page 29 [48]   The section commencing רַבִּי יִשְׁמָעֵאל אוֹמֵר will be incomprehensible, even in translation, to those uninitiated into Talmudic study. However, these 'Thirteen Principles of Rabbi Ishmael' are of paramount importance as a key to the way Biblical verses are to be analysed and compared with a view to deriving further laws from them.

page 31 [52]   After the 'Thirteen Principles of Rabbi Ishmael', the Reader recites aloud the יְהִי רָצוֹן, a prayer for the restoration of the Temple, after which the *Kaddish d'Rabbanan* (for transliteration, see pages 145 to 146) is recited by mourners. It is an expanded form of the ordinary 'Mourner's *Kaddish*' (קַדִּישׁ יָתוֹם), on page 35 (*Singer's*) and 52 (*ArtScroll*). The added paragraph is a petition for the welfare of Rabbis and students of the *Torah*.

This *Kaddish d'Rabbanan* is recited only when passages from Rabbinic literature have been read. These can be distinguished by their introductory source-headings which usually refer to *Mishnah*, *Beraita* or *Talmud*. This *Kaddish* is also recited as a conclusion to any discourse or *Shiur* given by the Rabbi. It is not recited after the sermon. The *Kaddish* is recited standing, with feet together, facing the Ark, and only when there is a *minyan* present.

page 33 [54-56]   The Reader recites aloud the opening verse of psalm 30, and the conclusion הָפַכְתָּ מִסְפְּדִי, ending with the words לְעוֹלָם אוֹדֶךָ. The mourners then recite the ordinary Mourner's *Kaddish*. This *Kaddish* is recited after psalms or prayers (as opposed to Rabbinic study passages). Having concluded the Mourner's *Kaddish*, the congregation - still standing - gather together the two front *Tzitzit* (fringes) of the *Tallit* which are held between the fingers while the blessing, בָּרוּךְ שֶׁאָמַר, is recited.

The function of בָּרוּךְ שֶׁאָמַר is to serve as a prologue, or introductory blessing, to the psalms which follow. This is clear from the wording of the blessing: "We also will praise thee, O Lord our God, with the songs of David Thy servant . . . ".

At the concluding words מֶלֶךְ מְהֻלָּל בַּתִּשְׁבָּחוֹת, the *Tzitzit* are kissed. The congregation then sits and recites silently the passage from הוֹדוּ לַייָ כִּי טוֹב to אָשִׁירָה לַייָ כִּי גָמַל עָלָי. The Reader breaks up this long selection of Biblical quotations by reciting aloud the following verses, as he reaches them.

page 39 [62] כִּי כָּל אֱלֹהֵי הָעַמִּים אֱלִילִים. וַייָ שָׁמַיִם עָשָׂה

page 39 [62] רוֹמְמוּ יְיָ אֱלֹהֵינוּ וְהִשְׁתַּחֲווּ לְהַר קָדְשׁוֹ
כִּי קָדוֹשׁ יְיָ אֱלֹהֵינוּ

page 41 [62] יְיָ צְבָאוֹת, אַשְׁרֵי אָדָם בֹּטֵחַ בָּךְ. יְיָ הוֹשִׁיעָה
הַמֶּלֶךְ יַעֲנֵנוּ בְיוֹם קָרְאֵנוּ

page 41 [64] יְהִי חַסְדְּךָ יְיָ עָלֵינוּ, כַּאֲשֶׁר יִחַלְנוּ לָךְ

page 41 [64] וַאֲנִי בְּחַסְדְּךָ בָטַחְתִּי, יָגֵל לִבִּי בִּישׁוּעָתֶךָ,
אָשִׁירָה לַייָ כִּי גָמַל עָלָי

page 41 [64] At the end of the above section, the congregation stands to recite psalm 100, מִזְמוֹר לְתוֹדָה. We stand (or open the Ark) principally for psalms, prayers or compositions that, for historical or theological reasons, were traditionally invested with importance.

Psalm 100, the Psalm of Thanksgiving, accompanied the offering of the Thanksgiving Sacrifice in Temple times. Unlike obligatory sacrifices or sin offerings, the

Thanksgiving was a voluntary expression of appreciation to God. As such, it was regarded as the most acceptable and valuable type of offering. This is reflected in the Rabbinic comment that "In the Messianic era all sacrifices will be suspended, except the Thanksgiving Sacrifice; and all prayers will be suspended, except for the Thanksgiving Prayer". In tribute to its importance, we stand while reciting it.

The psalm is not recited on those occasions mentioned in the rubric, because in Temple times the Thanksgiving Sacrifice was not brought on those days.

At this point on Sabbath and festivals,
additional psalms are recited -
Singer's, top of page 295: *ArtScroll* page 374.
See our commentary to the *Shabbat* morning service,
below, page 89 *ff.*

---

page 41 [64]   The congregation sits to recite the section commencing יְהִי כְבוֹד. Many Readers recite aloud the concluding three lines of this section, commencing וְהוּא רַחוּם, since they constitute a single unit which appears again at the commencement of the evening service (*Ma-ariv*) for week-days.

page 43 [66]   There now follows the recitation of the last six psalms of the Biblical Book of Psalms, commencing with psalm 145. The latter is prefaced by two verses:

אַשְׁרֵי הָעָם שֶׁכָּכָה לּוֹ and אַשְׁרֵי יוֹשְׁבֵי בֵיתֶךָ,

borrowed from another context, and ends with the verse וַאֲנַחְנוּ נְבָרֵךְ יָהּ. The Talmud considers these six psalms as an independent unit, to which the name *P'sukei d'Zimra*, 'Verses of Praise', was given.

It was customary among pietistic circles in early Talmudic times for worshippers to arrive at the synagogue an hour or so before the commencement of the Morning Service in order to meditate and prepare themselves spiritually for Prayer. It seems that they used to read the whole Book of Psalms at that time. When the 'ordinary' worshippers arrived, at the official time for the Morning Service, they would join in with the pietists in the recitation of the last few psalms. Hence, in the course of time, the recitation of the last six psalms of the Book of Psalms came to be regarded as an intrinsic part of the Morning Service.

The importance of אַשְׁרֵי may be inferred from the fact that we recite it three times daily. The Talmud even states that whoever recites it thrice daily can be assured of a place in heaven. The most important line of the psalm is undoubtedly:

פּוֹתֵחַ אֶת יָדֶךָ, וּמַשְׂבִּיעַ לְכָל חַי רָצוֹן

"Thou openest Thine hand, and satisfiest every living thing with favour". We indicate the importance of this line, which acknowledges the material bounty of God, by touching the boxes of the hand- and head-*Tefillin* with the fingers of our right hand and kissing them.

page 45 [68]   The Reader reads aloud from תְּהִלַּת יְיָ יְדַבֶּר פִּי until מֵעַתָּה וְעַד עוֹלָם, הַלְלוּיָהּ. He then proclaims aloud the first five words of the next psalm (146):

הַלְלוּיָהּ, הַלְלִי נַפְשִׁי אֶת יְיָ

and concludes with the last line:

page 47 [70]   יִמְלֹךְ יְיָ לְעוֹלָם אֱלֹהַיִךְ צִיּוֹן לְדֹר וָדֹר הַלְלוּיָהּ

page 47 [70]   The Reader proclaims aloud the first five words of the next psalm (147):

הַלְלוּיָהּ כִּי טוֹב זַמְּרָה אֱלֹהֵינוּ:

page 47 [72]   and concludes with the last three lines, commencing וּמִשְׁפָּטִים בַּל יְדָעוּם הַלְלוּיָהּ until מַגִּיד דְּבָרָיו.

He announces the next psalm (148) by proclaiming

the first six words: הַלְלוּיָהּ, הַלְלוּ אֶת יְיָ מִן הַשָּׁמַיִם concluding with the last three lines of the psalm, commencing וַיָּרֶם קֶרֶן לְעַמּוֹ. The same procedure is followed with the next psalm (149). The Reader announces the first five words:

page 49 [72]

הַלְלוּיָהּ שִׁירוּ לַיְיָ שִׁיר חָדָשׁ.

and the last two lines:

page 49 [74]

לַעֲשׂוֹת בָּהֶם מִשְׁפָּט כָּתוּב,
הָדָר הוּא לְכָל חֲסִידָיו הַלְלוּיָהּ.

The first four words of the last psalm (150) are announced, and the last verse,

page 51 [74]

כֹּל הַנְּשָׁמָה תְּהַלֵּל יָהּ הַלְלוּיָהּ

is repeated by the congregation and the Reader to indicate the final verse of the Book of Psalms.

The psalms are divided into five books, on the pattern of the Five Books of Moses, each book ending with a doxology or Praise of God. The doxologies that appear at the conclusion of the second and third books of the Psalms are contained in the next paragraph, from בָּרוּךְ יְיָ לְעוֹלָם, אָמֵן וְאָמֵן, to form a characteristic conclusion to the collection of six psalms just recited.

The congregation stands up for the recitation of the next five pages, from וַיְבָרֶךְ דָּוִיד until וּבוֹרֵא אֶת הַכֹּל (page 59 [84]). The former section is from I Chronicles 29: 10-13. It speaks of the occasion when King David's appeal for donations towards the building of the Temple met with a most overwhelming response on the part of the nation. David was deeply moved, and his intense pride found expression in the blessing of God contained in the וַיְבָרֶךְ דָּוִיד passage. From the previous Biblical chapter we learn that David had remained standing from the commencement of his appeal until the end of the blessing. Hence we stand while reciting it. The Reader does not recite aloud the concluding words of וַיְבָרֶךְ דָּוִיד, and the congregation does not pause, therefore, until the end of the following paragraph: וּמָצָאתָ אֶת לְבָבוֹ נֶאֱמָן לְפָנֶיךָ

page 51 [76]   The linking of the וַיְבָרֶךְ דָּוִיד passage with the section אַתָּה הוּא יְיָ לְבַדֶּךָ (Nehemiah 9: 6-11), is contextually logical, in that the latter section is also a blessing of the Almighty, similarly uttered in a standing position in the presence of the whole assembly of the nation. Both blessings were inspired by an act of sacrifice on the part of the nation. The nation's sacrifice in the time of David was financial, whereas in the time of Nehemiah it was personal and domestic, as well as religious. The Judean community, that had returned from exile in Babylon, in 537 BCE, assimilated and inter-married speedily, and forgot the *Torah*. Ezra and Nehemiah brought about a spiritual revival, though this entailed great sacrifice on the part of the Judeans, such as their having to divorce their heathen wives, refrain from doing business on the Sabbath, even in the face of an influx of foreign traders on that day, and, finally, to observe the seventh year as a year of release and rest for the land.

The Reader reads aloud the last three lines, commencing אַתָּה הוּא יְיָ הָאֱלֹהִים.

page 53 [76]   The paragraph commencing וְכָרוֹת עִמּוֹ הַבְּרִית is, in turn, contextually linked to the Song of the Red Sea which follows it. The Reader recites the last three lines of this paragraph, commencing וְהַיָּם בָּקַעְתָּ לִפְנֵיהֶם.

page 53 [78]   The Reader announces the first four words of the next paragraph, וַיּוֹשַׁע יְיָ בַּיּוֹם הַהוּא, concluding with the last line: וַיִּירְאוּ הָעָם אֶת יְיָ וַיַּאֲמִינוּ בַּיְיָ וּבְמֹשֶׁה עַבְדּוֹ.

The *Shirah* (Song of the Red Sea) is recited silently by the congregation. In Temple times, it was recited only on Sabbaths, when it was sung as an accompaniment

44

to the *Tamid*, the communal sacrifice. It ultimately became the practice to recite it daily throughout Israel. In Babylon and other centres of Jewry its recitation was not at all standardized. Maimonides makes reference to some communities which preferred to recite other songs, such as that of *Ha-aziynu* (Deuteronomy chapter 32).

page 57 [80]   At the end of the *Shirah*, the Reader recites aloud the three verses:

כִּי לַייָ הַמְּלוּכָה (Psalm 22:29)

וְעָלוּ מוֹשִׁעִים בְּהַר צִיּוֹן (Obadiah 1:21)

וְהָיָה יְיָ לְמֶלֶךְ עַל כָּל הָאָרֶץ (Zechariah 14: 9)

The purpose of these three verses is to substantiate the idea of Divine Kingship, contained in the final sentence of the *Shirah* ("The Lord shall reign for ever and ever"), with similar quotations from the other two divisions of the Bible: the Prophets and the Sacred Writings. In this way the inseparable unity of the Bible is demonstrated.

The *ArtScroll* and previous editions of *Singer's* add a final verse: וּבְתוֹרָתְךָ כָּתוּב לֵאמֹר. שְׁמַע יִשְׂרָאֵל. This was regarded by the Vilna Gaon as based on an incorrect scribal intrusion, from the *Rosh Hashanah Malchuyyot* verses, and is consequently not to be recited aloud by the Reader.

On *Shabbat* mornings
the Service continues with נִשְׁמַת.

(*Singer's* page 323; *ArtScroll*, page 400)

---

page 57 [82]   Where more than one mourner wishes to act as Reader, the second one takes over at this point, commencing with the words יִשְׁתַּבַּח שִׁמְךָ לָעַד מַלְכֵּנוּ. This paragraph is actually a concluding blessing over the psalms, and is consequently the counterpart of בָּרוּךְ שֶׁאָמַר, the blessing which introduced their recitation. The Reader recites aloud the last four lines, commencing: בְּרָכוֹת וְהוֹדָאוֹת מֵעַתָּה וְעַד עוֹלָם, until אֵל חֵי הָעוֹלָמִים, after which he recites the *Kaddish*.

This form of the *Kaddish* is a shortened one, and is known as חֲצִי קַדִּישׁ, the half-*Kaddish*. The Reader recites it again later in *Shacharit*, during the *Minchah* (Afternoon) Service and in the *Ma-ariv* (Evening) Service. Its primary function is to demarcate the end of one of the principal sections of the service. Here it serves to mark the conclusion of the *P'sukei d'Zimra*, the Hymns of Praise, and to indicate the beginning of the main part of the service.

page 59 [84] The Reader recites aloud: בָּרְכוּ אֶת יְיָ הַמְבֹרָךְ, bowing towards the Ark. The congregation, also bowing, responds with בָּרוּךְ יְיָ הַמְבֹרָךְ לְעוֹלָם וָעֶד. The Reader repeats this response and continues with the blessing:

בָּרוּךְ אַתָּה יְיָ...עֹשֶׂה שָׁלוֹם וּבוֹרֵא אֶת הַכֹּל.

When prayers are not said in the company of a *minyan*, the above two responsive verses are omitted. It is forbidden to speak after the recitation of *Bor'chu* until the end of the *Amidah*.

Regarding the section printed in *ArtScroll* and earlier editions of *Singer's*, on the left of *Bor'chu*, Israel Abrahams observes that "the practice of *Chazanim* to prolong the melody in singing the first words of *Bor'chu* is in part due to the desire to allow the congregation time for reciting that long response". The custom of reciting this passage has lapsed, however, in most synagogues.

The blessing יוֹצֵר אוֹר וּבוֹרֵא חֹשֶׁךְ . . . וּבוֹרֵא אֶת הַכֹּל ('who forms light ... and creates all things') is a quotation from Isaiah 45:7, though our Prayer Book

46

has amended the verse conspicuously. In Isaiah, the end of the verse reads עֹשֶׂה שָׁלוֹם וּבוֹרֵא רָע ('who makes peace and creates evil'). It has been suggested that Isaiah's reference to God as the Creator of evil was meant to act as a protest against the Persian dualistic religion which attributed good and evil to two separate deities, Ahuramazda (god of light and goodness) and Ahriman (god of darkness and evil). At a later period, when the force of the polemic had been defused, the designation of God as the Creator of evil was regarded as irreverent. The phrase וּבוֹרֵא אֶת הַכֹּל ('and creates all things') was therefore substituted.

While reciting this blessing it is customary to kiss the hand- and head-*Tefillin* with the fingers. This devotional act serves to underline the fact that this represents the commencement of the main part of the service for which it is obligatory to wear *Tefillin*.

The praise of God as Creator of light is expanded in the paragraph הַמֵּאִיר לָאָרֶץ, to embrace every aspect of nature. 'Even in times of direst oppression and misery, these prayers continued unchanged, and no outward suffering could dim the eye of the Jew to the wonders of Creation's renewal' (Sachs).

page 59-61
[84-86]

The next 18 lines (in both editions) are recited silently by the Reader and the congregation. The Reader then recites aloud from: וְכֻלָּם פּוֹתְחִים אֶת פִּיהֶם until וּמַעֲרִיצִים וּמַקְדִּישִׁים וּמַמְלִיכִים.

page 61 [86]

The top paragraph, אֵל בָּרוּךְ גָּדוֹל, constitutes an alphabetical acrostic. It continues the theme of light, paying special tribute to the health-giving rays of the sun. The next paragraph, תִּתְבָּרַךְ צוּרֵנוּ, is couched in a more mystical vein, referring to the heavenly beings who likewise offer praise to God.

The mystical theme is continued in the paragraph

47

commencing אֶת שֵׁם הָאֵל הַמֶּלֶךְ which leads into the *Kedushah*. The קָדוֹשׁ קָדוֹשׁ קָדוֹשׁ quotation, from Isaiah's vision, conveys the thought that the universe, allegorically described to include the angels of the celestial spheres, constitutes an incontrovertible testimony to the greatness of God.

The Reader recites the opening words: אֶת שֵׁם הָאֵל, followed by the last few lines of the paragraph, commencing לְהַקְדִּישׁ לְיוֹצְרָם. When the Reader has reached the word בְּיִרְאָה, the congregation recites aloud the line:

קָדוֹשׁ קָדוֹשׁ קָדוֹשׁ יְיָ צְבָאוֹת, מְלֹא כָל הָאָרֶץ כְּבוֹדוֹ.

This is repeated by the Reader.

page 61 [88]   The congregation then recites the paragraph commencing וְהָאוֹפַנִּים וְחַיּוֹת הַקֹּדֶשׁ until the words מְשַׁבְּחִים וְאוֹמְרִים. This is repeated by the Reader.

page 63 [88]   The congregation concludes by reciting aloud the words בָּרוּךְ כְּבוֹד יְיָ מִמְּקוֹמוֹ, which are repeated by the Reader. The congregation then recites silently the paragraph commencing לְאֵל בָּרוּךְ נְעִימוֹת יִתֵּנוּ. The Reader recites the concluding part of the blessing, commencing אוֹר חָדָשׁ עַל צִיּוֹן תָּאִיר, 'O cause a new light to shine upon Zion'.

The recital of this last phrase was criticised by the eminent leader of Babylonian Jewry, Saadiah Gaon, on the grounds that it constituted an unwarranted intrusion. He asserted that, since the function of the blessing is to thank God for the natural light of the sun, there is no justification for interrupting with an extraneous theme, petitioning for Messianic redemption, even though, metaphorically speaking, this may be described as a 'new light'.

The Reader recites aloud the first three words of the

next blessing: אַהֲבָה רַבָּה אֲהַבְתָּנוּ. This refers to the Divine love of Israel which was manifested especially through His giving of the *Torah* to her. We thank Him, therefore, for the physical light, referred to in the previous blessing, as well as for the rays of intellectual and moral light diffused by the *Torah*.

The worshipper, while reciting the phrase

וַהֲבִיאֵנוּ לְשָׁלוֹם מֵאַרְבַּע כַּנְפוֹת הָאָרֶץ,

"And bring us in peace from the four corners of the earth", gathers in his hands the *Tzitzit*, suspended from the *four corners* of his *Tallit*.

page 63 [90]   The Reader recites the last three lines of the blessing, commencing: וְקֵרַבְתָּנוּ לְשִׁמְךָ הַגָּדוֹל סֶלָה בֶּאֱמֶת.

page 67 [90]   <center>THE *SHEMA*</center>

The three paragraphs of the *Shema* are recited silently by the congregation until the words: יְיָ אֱלֹהֵיכֶם אֱמֶת. The *Shema* is prefaced by the words אֵל מֶלֶךְ נֶאֱמָן, the initial letters of which make up the word אָמֵן. In a number of early *Siddur* manuscripts we find that the previous blessing of אַהֲבָה רַבָּה actually concludes with the word אָמֵן. It is clear, therefore, that the phrase אֵל מֶלֶךְ נֶאֱמָן, although in appearance an introduction to the *Shema*, is, in fact, a conclusion of the previous section.

When reciting the line שְׁמַע יִשְׂרָאֵל it is customary to cover the eyes with the right hand. This serves as an aid to concentration on this most significant and fundamental affirmation of the absolute unity of God. It will be noticed that the three paragraphs of the *Shema* are provided with *n'ginot*, musical and punctuation notes for the Reading of the *Torah*. The reason is simply that these are Biblical passages, and strictly speaking, should be chanted in the prescribed

49

manner. The first paragraph of the *Shema* teaches that love of God should be all-embracing and selfless. "Heart, soul and might" are interpreted by our Sages to mean, respectively, passion, life and wealth. All these should be willingly surrendered in the higher service of God.

"And you shall teach them diligently to your children". To guarantee our survival, the religious education of our children must be our first priority.

page 67 [92]   When reciting the phrases: וּקְשַׁרְתָּם לְאוֹת עַל יָדֶךָ and וְהָיוּ לְטֹטָפֹת בֵּין עֵינֶיךָ, we touch the boxes of the hand- and head-*Tefillin*, respectively, and then kiss the hand. This devotional act emphasizes that we are joyfully fulfilling the *mitzvah* of *Tefillin* as prescribed by these verses.

The second paragraph of the *Shema* preaches the doctrine of reward and punishment. "But such reward, whether conceived as material blessing, or, as in later ages, when it became more and more spiritualized, is not made the motive for virtue. That must be love of God and His commandments, a free enthusiasm for doing His will" (Hertz).

page 69 [82]   The further reference to the *Tefillin* in the second paragraph of the *Shema* (*Singer's*, lines 2-3; *ArtScroll*, as indicated) is again highlighted by the devotional kiss with the hand. The word צִיצִת appears three times in the third paragraph. Each time the word is uttered, the *Tzitzit* are kissed.

page 69 [94]   The *Tzitzit* are kissed again on reaching the word אֱמֶת, and the Reader and congregation pause there until the Rabbi has completed the paragraph. The Rabbi usually recites aloud the whole of this paragraph, until the word אֱמֶת. This word rightfully belongs to the next paragraph, as printed in *Singer's*, since the Biblical *Shema* passage ends with the word אֱלֹהֵיכֶם. The *Mishnah* nevertheless prescribed that the word אֱמֶת be joined to the previous paragraph.

This regulation appears in the context of a discussion on the permissibility of interrupting to greet another while reciting the three paragraphs of the *Shema*. While the *Mishnah* is more lenient regarding interruptions, under certain circumstances, between paragraphs, yet Rabbi Judah's view was respected that at the end of the third paragraph he should not interrupt until he has recited the word אֱמֶת. Rabbi Judah's extension of the paragraph, by the addition of the single word אֱמֶת, is based on the fact that the phrase וַיְיָ אֱלֹהֵיכֶם אֱמֶת occurs in Jeremiah 10: 10. To begin a new paragraph with the word אֱמֶת would constitute, in Rabbi Judah's view, an abbreviation of the Jeremiah phrase, which could not be sanctioned.

The section אֱמֶת וְיַצִּיב is an emphatic declaration of the permanent validity of the Law. Note the succession of adjectives descriptive of the *Torah*. Such hyperbole was employed only for polemical reasons, to counter heretical views. It was possibly inspired by the Christian view that the Law had lost its binding authority once the New Testament had been revealed.

page 71 [94] The phrase וּמַלְכוּתוֹ וֶאֱמוּנָתוֹ לָעַד קַיֶּמֶת is said aloud by the Reader. On reaching the word קַיֶּמֶת the *Tzitzit* are kissed. They are kissed again after the phrase וּלְעוֹלְמֵי עוֹלָמִים, and are put away at the end of the paragraph. The Reader reads aloud the last three lines of the paragraph, from עַל אֲבוֹתֵינוּ until יִשְׂרָאֵל עֲבָדֶיךָ.

The Reader announces the first four words of the next paragraph: עַל הָרִאשׁוֹנִים וְעַל הָאַחֲרוֹנִים, and ends with the last two lines:

פּוֹדֵנוּ וּמַצִּילֵנוּ מֵעוֹלָם הוּא שְׁמֶךָ. אֵין אֱלֹהִים זוּלָתֶךָ:

51

Service for Weekday Mornings

page 71 [96]   The Reader announces the first five words of the last paragraph: עֶזְרַת אֲבוֹתֵינוּ אַתָּה הוּא מֵעוֹלָם.

This passage, ending with: בָּרוּךְ אַתָּה יְיָ גָּאַל יִשְׂרָאֵל ("Blessed are thou, O Lord, who has redeemed Israel"), is referred to in the Talmud as the *G'ulah*, the Redemption Blessing. It is an expression of gratitude for the redemption from Egypt and the many miracles associated with that event, as well as for the constancy of Divine faithfulness to Israel throughout history.

page 73 [96]   The Reader reads the last three lines of the paragraph, commencing תְּהִלּוֹת לְאֵל עֶלְיוֹן. At that point, the congregation rises in preparation for the *Amidah*.

The congregation responds aloud with the two lines commencing מִי כָמֹכָה בָּאֵלִם יְיָ, until עֹשֵׂה פֶלֶא. This is repeated by the Reader. It is an extract from the Song of the Red Sea and signifies the grateful recognition by Israel of all God's kindnesses on her behalf.

The congregation and the Reader then recite alternately שִׁירָה חֲדָשָׁה until וְאָמְרוּ, together with the line יְיָ יִמְלֹךְ לְעֹלָם וָעֶד, followed by the paragraph בָּרוּךְ אַתָּה יְיָ. גָּאַל יִשְׂרָאֵל, until צוּר יִשְׂרָאֵל.

When reciting the latter blessing, the Reader lowers his voice to inaudibility. This is in order that the congregation should not recite *Amen* after this blessing, in fulfilment of the Talmudic regulation requiring that there should be no interruption between the blessing for redemption and the *Amidah*.

THE *AMIDAH*

page 75 [98]   *Amidah*, means 'standing prayer'. The worshipper should stand, with feet together facing the Ark, while reciting the *Amidah* silently. It is also known as the *Sh'moneh Esrei* ('Eighteen Blessings'), a title descriptive

52

of the original form of the prayer, though in our version
there are actually nineteen blessings. An indication of
the premier importance of the *Amidah* is gained by the
fact that it is consistently referred to in Talmudic writing
as *Tefillah*, 'The Prayer', par excellence.

It is forbidden to talk, or even to move one's feet, until
the end of the *Amidah*. Late-comers should not attempt,
therefore, to take their seats by pushing past those who
are still praying their silent *Amidah* - or who are in the
middle of the *Kedushah* in the Reader's repetition. They
should wait until these prayers are completed.

Before beginning the *Amidah* one should take three
steps backwards, commencing with the right foot,
followed by three steps forwards. The worshipper bows
towards the Ark when reciting the opening three words
of the first blessing: בָּרוּךְ אַתָּה יְיָ, as well as at its
concluding words: בָּרוּךְ אַתָּה יְיָ, מָגֵן אַבְרָהָם. Between
Rosh Hashanah and *Yom Kippur* only, we insert the lines
לְמַעַנְךָ אֱלֹהִים חַיִּים until זָכְרֵנוּ לַחַיִּים, (in smaller print).

The line מַשִּׁיב הָרוּחַ וּמוֹרִיד הַגֶּשֶׁם ("Who causes wind to
blow and rain to fall") is recited throughout the winter
months, commencing on the eighth day of the festival of
Sukkot (*Sh'miniy Atzeret*) and terminating on the first
day of *Pesach*.

page 77 [100] The congregation, when reciting the silent *Amidah*,
omits the *Kedushah*, that is from נְקַדֵּשׁ אֶת שִׁמְךָ בָּעוֹלָם,
until בָּרוּךְ אַתָּה יְיָ הָאֵל הַקָּדוֹשׁ.

page 79 [102] The blessing סְלַח לָנוּ is in the form of a confession and a
plea for pardon. It is customary to beat gently on the
breast with the right hand while reciting the phrases:
כִּי פָשָׁעְנוּ and כִּי חָטָאנוּ.

page 79 [104] The private prayer for a sick friend or relative (printed at
the foot of the page in both *Singer's* and *ArtScroll*) is not

Service for Weekday Mornings

an intrinsic part of the *Amidah*. The Hebrew name of the person we are praying for is inserted into the last line; and in this situation we use the Hebrew name of the mother (for example: *Mosheh ben Sarah*). After reciting this insertion, continue:

כִּי אֵל מֶלֶךְ רוֹפֵא נֶאֱמָן וְרַחֲמָן אָתָּה.
בָּרוּךְ אַתָּה יְיָ רוֹפֵא חוֹלֵי עַמּוֹ יִשְׂרָאֵל.

Note the special Reader's insertion (עֲנֵנוּ) for Fast Days. In the case of the congregation, its recitation is delayed until *Minchah*, as there is always a doubt whether or not the individual will feel strong enough to complete the fast. By *Minchah*, however, we assume that he will do so.

page 81 [104] The phrase וְתֵן בְּרָכָה עַל פְּנֵי הָאֲדָמָה ("And give a blessing on the face of the earth") is recited throughout the summer period, from *Pesach* until the 4th or 5th of December. From then until *Pesach*, the winter period, the phrase וְתֵן טַל וּמָטָר לִבְרָכָה עַל פְּנֵי הָאֲדָמָה ("And give dew and rain for a blessing...") is substituted.

page 83 [108] We have just referred to prayers for sick people that may be inserted into a blessing. Any personal petition for other pressing needs, such as livelihood, may be inserted into the blessing *Shema kohleinu*. *ArtScroll* includes such a prayer on this page.

page 83 [110] The section in smaller type, the יַעֲלֶה וְיָבֹא prayer, is inserted on all festivals (including *Rosh Chodesh*) into the *Amidah*, as well as into the Grace after Meals. On ordinary week-days continue with וְתֶחֱזֶינָה עֵינֵינוּ.

page 85 [112] During the silent *Amidah* the congregation recites the right-hand version of the מוֹדִים prayer, up to the words מֵעוֹלָם קִוִּינוּ לָךְ. When reciting the first three words, מוֹדִים אֲנַחְנוּ לָךְ, the worshipper bows towards the Ark.

page 87 [114] Except on *Chanukah* and *Purim*, when the עַל הַנִּסִּים verse, followed by the appropriate section, is recited, the

54

congregation continues with וְעַל כֻּלָּם.

page 87 [116]   The worshipper bows again when reciting the words בָּרוּךְ אַתָּה יְיָ, הַטּוֹב שִׁמְךָ. The second of these paragraphs, אֱלֹהֵינוּ וֵאלֹהֵי אֲבוֹתֵינוּ, is omitted during the silent recitation of the Amidah.

page 89 [118]   When reciting the last three lines of עֹשֶׂה שָׁלוֹם, the worshipper takes three steps backwards, bows to the left, then to the right, followed by three steps forwards.

Distraction during Prayer

If one became distracted during the recitation of the Amidah, or, when praying by heart, he became confused as to which blessing he was up to, if he knew that he was somewhere in the middle of the *first* three blessings, he should re-commence the Amidah. If he knew that he was in the middle of the *last* three blessings, he should return to the *Retzei*. If he knew that he had been distracted while reciting the intermediate blessings, he should return to the first of those blessings that he feels sure he has not recited (*Chayyei Adam* 24: 21).

THE REPETITION OF THE *AMIDAH*

It is customary for the Reader to wait for the Rabbi to complete his recitation of the Amidah before commencing the repetition. The Reader reads in a loud, distinct voice, pausing for a moment in each blessing, after reciting the phrase בָּרוּךְ אַתָּה יְיָ, in order enable the congregation to respond with בָּרוּךְ הוּא וּבָרוּךְ שְׁמוֹ, as well as after the last word of each blessing, to enable the congregation to respond with אָמֵן. When prayers are not recited in the presence of a *minyan*, the Amidah is not repeated.

page 77 [100]   The *Kedushah* is recited alternately, by the Reader and

55

Service for Weekday Mornings

congregation, during the repetition of the *Amidah*. The Reader waits for the congregation to recite the first three lines of the *Kedushah,* until וְקָרָא זֶה אֶל זֶה וְאָמַר, before he repeats it. The congregation recites aloud the next two lines, from קָדוֹשׁ קָדוֹשׁ קָדוֹשׁ ("Holy, Holy, Holy") until מְלֹא כָל הָאָרֶץ כְּבוֹדוֹ, which the Reader repeats.

The Reader then continues לְעֻמָּתָם בָּרוּךְ יֹאמֵרוּ, and the congregation responds: בָּרוּךְ כְּבוֹד יְיָ מִמְּקוֹמוֹ. This is repeated by the Reader, who then continues with the words וּבְדִבְרֵי קָדְשְׁךָ כָּתוּב לֵאמֹר. The congregation responds with יִמְלֹךְ יְיָ, which is repeated by the Reader, who then continues with לְדֹר וָדֹר, until the end of the blessing.

page 79 [104]   On Fast Days the reader adds עֲנֵנוּ.

page 85 [112]   The Reader says מוֹדִים aloud, while the congregation recite their own version of this blessing - called *Modim d'Rabbanan* - in an undertone.

On *Chanukah* and *Purim* the Reader recites aloud the עַל הַנִסִּים prayer, and the appropriate accompanying section.

page 87 [116]   The Reader recites aloud the paragraph commencing אֱלֹהֵינוּ וֵאלֹהֵי אֲבוֹתֵינוּ. It is omitted, however, in a house of mourning. This passage contains the Priestly Blessing of the congregation, recited daily in Temple times. In Israel this practice is preserved. The priests remove their shoes and have their hands washed by the Levites before ascending to the Ark. The Reader pauses after reciting each of the three final phrases:

יְבָרֶכְךָ יְיָ וְיִשְׁמְרֶךָ.
יָאֵר יְיָ פָּנָיו אֵלֶיךָ וִיחֻנֶּךָּ.
יִשָּׂא יְיָ פָּנָיו אֵלֶיךָ וְיָשֵׂם לְךָ שָׁלוֹם.

thereby giving the congregation time to utter the

response כֵּן יְהִי רָצוֹן, after each phrase. The Reader concludes with the blessing:

בָּרוּךְ אַתָּה יְיָ, הַמְבָרֵךְ אֶת עַמּוֹ יִשְׂרָאֵל בַּשָּׁלוֹם.

He does not recite the אֱלֹהַי נְצוֹר, and no *Kaddish* is recited here (except on those days when *Tachanun* is omitted).

page 93 [120]

On Fast Days and during the Ten Days of Penitence, the Ark is opened and אָבִינוּ מַלְכֵּנוּ is recited after the Reader's repetition of the *Amidah*. It is recited silently, but the congregation waits, after reaching the line:

מְחוֹק בְּרַחֲמֶיךָ הָרַבִּים כָּל שִׁטְרֵי חוֹבוֹתֵינוּ,

for the Reader to lead them in a responsive recitation of the next nine lines. During the Ten Days of Penitence, we add the word בְּסֵפֶר, ("in the book of"), in the spirit of the central theme of that period when God opens before Him the books of life and prosperity, death and adversity.

On semi-holy days, such as *Rosh Chodesh*, the intermediate days of *Pesach* and *Sukkot* (*Chol ha-Mo-ed*) as well as on *Chanukah*, the Reader commences immediately with *Hallel* (*Singer's*, page 585: *ArtScroll*, page 632), after which *Kaddish* is said. The service then continues with the Reading of the Law.

TACHANUN

page 99 [124]

Tachanun means 'petition, intercesion'. It originated in Temple times, when an opportunity for private, spontaneous petition was offered to the worshipper once the *Tamid*, the main Morning Sacrifice, had been completed and the priests had blessed all those present. At the utterance of the Divine name in the Priestly Blessing, the people would fall on their knees and prostrate themselves fully on the ground as a mark of reverence. And it was in that pose, pressed against the ground as an expression of total worthlessness, that the worshipper could pour out his heart, his needs and complaints to God.

From the Temple context, the *Tachanun* entered the synagogue, and ultimately became a casualty of the latter's preference for formulated public worship, rather than private meditation. Thus, the vacuum was filled by composed recitations of confessions (*Viddui*), prayers for forgiveness (*Selichot*), lament over the loss of the Temple, the iniquity of the nation and the nothingness of man. Its original status, as an optional, meditative interlude, was still preserved, however, for many centuries, to the extent that the Babylonian *Geonim* (8th to 12th century) readily offered people the choice of reciting their own petitions at that point in the service. This situation continued until the period of the *Shulchan Aruch* (16th century), which still describes the recitation of the *Tachanun* composition as a mere custom. The only remaining relic of its former status as a private composition lies in the fact that it is not led by the Reader, but recited individually as a private petition.

Although in Maimonides' day (12th century), the custom in several communities was still to prostrate oneself fully on the ground, yet already this was being more generally replaced by a token leaning on the arm. The left arm is regarded as the weaker one, which, for the recitation of a composition highlighting Israel's weakness, was regarded as the more appropriate. Hence, for the

Tachanun recited during the *Minchah* service we recline on that arm. During the *Shacharit* service, however, when we have the *Tefillin* on our left arm, it was not regarded as respectful to lean on them, for which reason we lean for that service on our right arm. We commence leaning at וַיֹּאמֶר דָּוִד אֶל גָּד (*page* 105 [132]), until the phrase יָשְׁבוּ יַבְשׁוּ רָגַע (*page* 134 [105]).

Another halachic regulation, which recalls the origin of this section of the service as deriving from the Temple prostrations, is that we lean on the arm only when praying *Tachanun* inside a synagogue, regarded by the Rabbis as 'the Temple in miniature'. When praying at home, or in a room that has no Ark containing a scroll of the Law, *Tachanun* is recited in the usual sitting position.

In Talmudic times, Mondays and Thursdays were especially designated for Fast Days by pietistic groups wishing to mourn the loss of the Temple. Public fasting during periods of drought was also always prescribed for those days. They were generally also the market days, and the people from the villages would come to the market towns and, before embarking on their trading, would listen to the *Torah* being read and participate in the public worship. Hence, on Mondays and Thursdays, extra *Tachanunim* were recited - introduced probably by the pietists who were observing those days as Fast Days - which explains why that section of our prayers is considerably expanded on those days.

Some communities have the practice that *Tachanun* is dispensed with if a boy is present in synagogue on the weekday when he becomes *Barmitzvah* and puts on his *Tefillin* for the first time. The rationale is that the addition of a new adult Jew to the ranks of the community means that the *mitzvot* he performs accrue not only to his own merit, but also to that of the community at large. It is therefore a *Yom Tov* for all present; and on a *Yom Tov* we do not recite *Tachanun.* This is because its basic theme, that of Israel's abject state of unworthiness, sinfulness, persecution, loss of her Temple and need for God's mercy and redemption, was considered as impairing the joy of the festival.

Rav Ovadiah Yosef, former Sephardi Chief Rabbi of Israel, strongly commends the omission of *Tachanun* on such an occasion (see *Yechaveh Da-at* II, page 66), regarding its joy as equivalent to that of a bridegroom in synagogue on his wedding day, when *Tachanun* is similarly omitted. He adds that this has become more and more the practice in synagogues in Jerusalem over recent years.

It has to be said that other authorities do not agree that *Tachanun* should be omitted for such an event, for the simple reason that this was not included by the *Shulchan Aruch* in its list of days when *Tachanun* is omitted. Another argument is that there is no guarantee that this particular *Barmitzvah* boy will indeed continue with his religious observances, and be a credit and joy to the community!

Rabbi Chayim David Halevi discusses the pros and cons of this question in his celebrated work, *Asei Lecha Rav* (VI, pages 37-42), and concludes that "each community may follow its own practice, as it deems appropriate".

Tachanun is omitted in a house of mourning; if a bridegroom is present in synagogue during the entire week of his wedding; if the *mohel*, the father of the child or the *Sandek* of a circumcision to be held later in the day are present in synagogue, as well as on other festive semi-holydays listed in the rubrics of the prayer book.

The longest period when *Tachanun* is omitted is the entire month of *Nisan*. This is because, in the desert, it was during the first twelve days of *Nisan* that each of the twelve princes was installed into office, and offered a festive, Thanksgiving Sacrifice. Add to this the day before *Pesach*, which had a festive spirit, plus the seven (or eight Diaspora) days of *Pesach*, and *Isru Chag* (the day after a major festival), which is also a festive aftermath, and we have the majority of the month of *Nisan* as festive days. The Rabbis applied to this the principle that the majority imposes its spirit on the entire month.

After concluding the *Tachanun,* the Reader recites the half-*Kaddish,* and on Sundays, Tuesdays, Wednesdays and Fridays he continues with אַשְׁרֵי יוֹשְׁבֵי בֵיתֶךָ. On Mondays and Thursdays the congregation recites the two paragraphs commencing אֵל אֶרֶךְ אַפַּיִם.

page 113 [138] THE READING OF THE *TORAH*

On Mondays and Thursdays the *Sefer Torah* is taken out, three people are called up and the first portion of the *Sidrah* for the following *Shabbat* is read. These two days were, as we have observed, market days in ancient Judea, and the practice was introduced of reading the *Torah* publicly in the market square on these days for the benefit of visiting traders and especially country folk who might live in remote parts where there was no opportunity of hearing the *Torah* read on *Shabbat.* The number of mid-week occasions on which the *Torah* was read was subsequently increased to include *Rosh Chodesh,* the intermediate days of festivals (*Chol ha-Mo-ed*), *Chanukah, Purim* and Fast Days. Tradition attributes the innovation of reading the *Torah* on Mondays and Thursdays to Ezra the Scribe (ca 400 BCE).

page 113 [140] The Ark is opened and the congregation recites the paragraph וַיְהִי בִּנְסוֹעַ. When the Reader has received the *Sefer Torah,* he rests it against his right shoulder and recites aloud גַּדְּלוּ לַיָי אִתִּי, וּנְרוֹמְמָה שְׁמוֹ יַחְדָּו. While the *Torah* is being carried to the *Bimah* the congregation and Reader recite לְךָ יְיָ הַגְּדֻלָּה and אַב הָרַחֲמִים.

page 115 [142] The Reader recites aloud the paragraph commencing וְתִגָּלֶה וְתֵרָאֶה, which constitutes an invitation to the *Cohen* (Priest) to ascend the *Bimah* in order to 'render honour to the law'. The first two *Aliyyot* (singular: *Aliyah*

61

- honour of being 'called up' to the Reading of the *Torah*) are given to a *Cohen* followed by a Levite. After these, any Israelite may be 'called up', though an order of priorities is prescribed where several members claim an obligation to be called up to mark a particular occasion or anniversary.

On being called up for an Aliyah

One makes one's way to the reading desk by the shortest route, in order to demonstrate eagerness to perform the *Mitzvah*. On returning to one's seat after being called up, a longer route is taken, normally shaking hands with the Wardens and members of the congregation, in order to indicate reluctance to leave the *Torah*. For the same reason it is our practice for a person to remain at the reading desk until the one who is called up immediately after him has recited his own concluding blessing over the *Torah*.

On arrival at the reading desk the one called up stands on the *right* side of the *Ba-al K'riah*, 'the one performing the Reading of the Law'. When the latter has indicated the place from which he will commence reading, the person called up places the edge of his *Tallit* upon that place, then kisses the *Tallit* before reciting the blessing - given in transliteration on page 152.

While the portion of the *Torah* is being read, the person called up holds the handle of the right hand *Etz Chayyim* (wooden stave) of the scroll. If he is familiar with the text, and can follow the *Ba-al K'riah*, he should read the portion with him, word for word, in an inaudible voice.

After the reading, the concluding blessing is recited - given in transliteration on page 152.

One should inform the Warden or synagogue office, as far as possible in advance, if one wishes to be called up to the *Torah* because of a special family occasion, such as a birth, an anniversary, a *Yahrzeit*, or in order to recite the blessing of *Gohmeil*. (The synagogue office usually retains a record of the dates when members observe *Yahrzeit* for their close relatives, and circularizes them accordingly).

The Gohmeil blessing

Gohmeil is a thanksgiving blessing for those who have been saved from a serious danger to life, or who have emerged from a situation of potential peril. It is generally recited by people who have recovered from a serious illness, accident or operation, and by those who have arrived safely after a journey by air or sea.

Immediately after the concluding blessing over the *Torah*, the formula of the *Gohmeil* is recited:

בָּרוּךְ אַתָּה, יְיָ אֱלֹהֵינוּ, מֶלֶךְ הָעוֹלָם,
הַגּוֹמֵל לְחַיָּבִים טוֹבוֹת, שֶׁגְּמָלַנִי כָּל טוֹב.

The congregation respond with:

מִי שֶׁגְּמָלְךָ כָּל טוֹב, הוּא יִגְמָלְךָ כָּל טוֹב סֶלָה

These blessings are given in transliteration on page 153.

Priorities for an Aliyah

The number of people called to the Reading of the *Torah* is regulated by tradition in accordance with the relative degree of sanctity of that particular day. On the most sacred of our holy days, the *Shabbat*, we call the highest number, seven. On *Yom Kippur* morning we call six; on the festivals five; on *Rosh Chodesh* and *Chol ha-Mo-ed* four; and on ordinary Mondays and Thursdays, *Shabbat* afternoons, *Chanukah* and *Purim*, we call three.

Even though it is permitted to call up more than the prescribed seven on *Shabbat* mornings, we are mindful of the prohibition against *tircha d'tzibbura*, making the service irksome to the community by a protracted Reading of the Law. We should endeavour, therefore, to establish a maximum calling of ten *Aliyyot.*

In large synagogues, with more than that number of congregants frequently celebrating special occasions, such as *Barmitzvah* boys and their families, *Yahrzeits, aufruf,* (bridegroom on the *Shabbat* before his wedding) and births, it proves necessary to establish an order of precedence so as to avoid contention where a Warden has to limit the list. The accepted order of priority is:

i.   A bridegroom on the day of his wedding.
ii.   A bridegroom on the *Shabbat* before his wedding.
iii. A *Barmitzvah* boy.
iv.   A father celebrating the birth of a child.
v.   A bridegroom on the *Shabbat* after his wedding.
vi.   A *Yahrzeit* for a parent occurring on that *Shabbat.*
vii. A *Yahrzeit* during the following week.
viii. One who has recovered from an illness.
ix.   One leaving for, or returning from, a journey abroad.
x.   A visitor to the synagogue.

Communities were particular to avoid arousing feelings of jealousy or ill-will in the hearts of the simple-minded at the spectacle of a number of members of the same family being called up in succession. However irrational this might seem to be, the custom has been maintained of not calling up two brothers or step-brothers, one after the other, nor a father followed by his son or grandson. On those special occasions when a second scroll is taken out for *Maftir,* there is not the same objection to calling up one member of the family for the final *Aliyah* of the first scroll and his close relatives (son, brother or step-brother) to *Maftir* from the second scroll.

After the prescribed number of people have been called up to the Reading of the *Torah,* the half-*Kaddish* is recited by the *Ba-al K'riah.*

page 119 [146]   Two men are then called-up: the first for *Hagbahah,* the

64

lifting up of the *Sefer Torah*; the second for *G'lilah*, the rolling and dressing of the Scroll. The *Torah* is lifted up, with at least three columns visible to the congregation, and the verse וְזֹאת הַתּוֹרָה (top line) is recited. During *G'lilah*, the Reader recites aloud the יְהִי רָצוֹן petitions. The congregation joins in the recitation of the last paragraph: אַחֵינוּ כָּל בֵּית יִשְׂרָאֵל. These petitions are omitted on days when *Tachanun* is not recited (see above, page 60).

The person honoured with *Hagbahah* should ascertain beforehand exactly where to sit down after raising the Scroll aloft. The one performing *G'lilah* should remember that the right-hand roller (*Etz Chayyim*) should be lifted over the left-hand roller. However, since the back of the *Torah* Scroll will be facing him as he stands to dress it, this means that his left-hand roller should be raised above his right-hand roller. Also, if it is a *Shabbat* morning, he should ascertain whether the one doing *Hagbahah* continues to hold the Scroll throughout the reading of the *Haftarah*, and until the prayer for the Royal Family or Government, or whether the *Torah* is placed in a special supporting niche during that time. In some synagogues it is only the one who performs *Hagbahah* who stays on the *Bimah* and follows the Scroll around the synagogue in procession until it is put away. Clarify the particular procedure in your synagogue if you expect to be called for these honours.

page 121 [148] The Reader receives the Scroll, rests it against his right shoulder and recites aloud:

יְהַלְלוּ אֶת שֵׁם יְיָ, כִּי נִשְׂגָּב שְׁמוֹ לְבַדּוֹ.

Congregation and Reader recite הוֹדוֹ and לְדָוִד מִזְמוֹר, in an audible voice. As the Scroll is being placed in the Ark, the Reader proclaims: וּבְנֻחֹה יֹאמַר.

The Reader recites aloud the last line: הֲשִׁיבֵנוּ, until כְּקֶדֶם, and the Ark is closed. The Reader walks back to

65

page 123 [150] the *Bimah* and announces the first line of אַשְׁרֵי. In many congregations the honour of acting as Reader is divided up further and another person takes over at this point.

page 125 [152] The Reader reads aloud from תְּהִלַּת יְיָ יְדַבֶּר פִּי, until הַלְלוּיָהּ. The rubric which follows specifies those occasions when the next psalm (20) is omitted.

page 127 [152] The Reader recites aloud the last two lines of the psalm, from הֵמָּה כָּרְעוּ וְנָפָלוּ, until בְּיוֹם קָרְאֵנוּ. He then announces the first line of the וּבָא לְצִיּוֹן prayer.

page 129 [156] The whole of this prayer is recited silently by the congregation. The Reader recites aloud the last three lines of the prayer, from וְיִבְטְחוּ בְךָ יוֹדְעֵי שְׁמֶךָ, until יַגְדִּיל תּוֹרָה וְיַאְדִּיר.

The original function of the וּבָא לְצִיּוֹן section was to serve as a Messianic conclusion to a lecture or study circle. From a 9th century Rabbinic source we learn that it was an ancient custom for students and scholars to remain behind in the synagogue after the conclusion of the service in order to hear a lecture and conduct a study group. They would conclude the lecture by reciting verses of consolation from the books of the Prophets, dealing with the theme of the Messianic redemption.

The passage וּבָא לְצִיּוֹן ("And a redeemer shall come to Zion" [Isaiah 59: 20]), was a particularly popular choice, in view of the fact that they applied the second verse, וּדְבָרַי אֲשֶׁר שַׂמְתִּי בְּפִיךָ ("And My words which I have put in your mouth"), to the *Torah* which they had just studied, the merit of which, they believed, would hasten the redemption. When, as a result of persecution or economic necessity, it was no longer possible to remain behind in synagogue for a study circle, the practice of reciting the selected verses remained.

It has been suggested by some authorities that the

66

Kedushah verse, קָדוֹשׁ קָדוֹשׁ קָדוֹשׁ (Isaiah 6: 3), was included for the benefit of the late-comers to the synagogue who may have missed its recitation during the service (Abudarham).

Three of the Biblical verses in this prayer are translated into Aramaic:

זִיו יְקָרֵהּ until וּמְקַבְּלִין דֵּן מִן דֵּן;
בֵּית שְׁכִינְתֵּהּ until וּנְטַלְתַּנִי רוּחָא;
יְיָ מַלְכוּתֵהּ קָאֵם לְעָלַם וּלְעָלְמֵי עָלְמַיָּא and.

These renderings acted as a substitute for the study of Talmud after the service. The early association of the וּבָא לְצִיּוֹן with study circles may also be detected in the second half of the passage commencing

בָּרוּךְ אֱלֹהֵינוּ שֶׁבְּרָאָנוּ לִכְבוֹדוֹ,

which is simply a benediction over *Torah* study.

The Talmud actually refers to the וּבָא לְצִיּוֹן section by the name *Kedushah d'Sidrah,* 'the *Kedushah* recited over a discourse', and an echo of its original function is still heard in the practice of some old style *Maggidim* (preachers) to end their discourses with the petition: וּבָא לְצִיּוֹן גּוֹאֵל וְנֹאמַר אָמֵן.

On *Rosh Chodesh*, the *Tefillin* are taken off at the end of the וּבָא לְצִיּוֹן section. The Reader recites the half-*Kaddish*, after which the congregation says the silent *Musaf Amidah* for *Rosh Chodesh*, (*page* 595 [644]).

In the section commencing אֱלֹהֵינוּ וֵאלֹהֵי אֲבוֹתֵינוּ (599 [648]), there are twelve Divine gifts listed:

לְטוֹבָה וְלִבְרָכָה. לְשָׂשׂוֹן וּלְשִׂמְחָה. לִישׁוּעָה וּלְנֶחָמָה. לְפַרְנָסָה וּלְכַלְכָּלָה. לְחַיִּים וּלְשָׁלוֹם. לִמְחִילַת חֵטְא. וְלִסְלִיחַת עָוֹן.

These correspond to the twelve months of the year. In a leap year, when we have an added month, we add an extra expression: וּלְכַפָּרַת פֶּשַׁע.

On *Chol ha-Mo-ed*, the *Musaf* for festivals is said (*page* 639 [674]).

The *Amidah* is repeated by the Reader, and sung to a distinctive *Yom Tov* melody.

page 131 [156]   The Reader recites *Kaddish Shaleim* ("Full-*Kaddish*"), also called *Kaddish Titkabbal,* after the first word of the added line:

תִּתְקַבַּל צְלוֹתְהוֹן וּבָעוּתְהוֹן דִּי כָל בֵּית יִשְׂרָאֵל קֳדָם
אֲבוּהוֹן דִּי בִשְׁמַיָּא וְאִמְרוּ אָמֵן

He then proclaims the opening words of the *Aleinu* prayer: עָלֵינוּ לְשַׁבֵּחַ.

page 133 [158]   The popularity of *Aleinu* is apparent from the fact that, since the 14th century, it has occupied an honoured position as the concluding prayer for all statutory services. It was originally composed by the Babylonian Talmudist, Rav, as an introduction to the *Malchuyyot* recited during the *Rosh Hashanah Amidah.* Its introduction was prompted because it won the hearts of the saintly martyrs of Franco-Germany who chose it as their dying song. By reciting this prayer three times daily we acknowledge our debt to our martyrs who, in every age, have given their lives so that Israel might survive.

page 135 [160]   The Reader concludes with the final two lines, from וְנֶאֱמַר וְהָיָה, after which mourners recite *Kaddish.*

page 137-143 [162-118]   The service concludes with the *Shir shel yom,* psalm for the day of the week. The Reader announces the first line of the particular psalm which specifies the current day of

68

page 145 [170]   the week. He concludes by reciting the last verse of the psalm, after which the mourners recite *Kaddish*. During the whole month of *Ellul*, and up to *Sh'miniy Atzeret*, psalm 27 is said here, after which mourners recite *Kaddish*.

page 461 [172]   On *Rosh Chodesh*, בָּרְכִי נַפְשִׁי is added, after which mourners recite *Kaddish*. On *Chanukah*, psalm 30 is said here (*page* 33 [54]), after which mourners recite *Kaddish*.

page 819 [808]   In a house of mourning, the Rabbi leads the assembly in the recitation of psalm 49, after which the mourner recites *Kaddish*. The Rabbi recites the Memorial prayer, after which the mourner again recites *Kaddish*.

The *Tefillin* are taken off at the end of the service, but one may begin taking them off after the וּבָא לְצִיּוֹן section.

The straps around the fingers are unwound. The head-*Tefillin* is then removed, wrapped up and replaced in the bag. Finally, the hand-*Tefillin* is unwound, wrapped up and replaced in the bag, in such a way that it comes to hand first, ready to be put on, the following morning.

It is not respectful to rush out of synagogue. On the contrary, one should leave slowly in order to symbolise the reluctance of parting.

69

Service for Weekday Afternoons
תְּפִלַּת מִנְחָה לַחוֹל

According to the *Talmud,* each of our Patriarchs introduced a special daily service. Abraham was responsible for the introduction of a morning service (*Shacharit*), Isaac introduced an afternoon service (*Minchah*) and Jacob an evening service (*Ma-ariv*).

In Temple times, the emphasis was rather on the offering of sacrifices, and two statutory offerings were made each day: a Morning Perpetual Offering (*Tamid Shel Shachar*), and an Early-Evening Perpetual Offering (*Tamid Shel Bein Ha-arbayim*). When the second Temple was destroyed by the Romans, in the year 70 CE, sacrifices were discontinued and replaced by prayers which reflected the content of the sacrificial system, and which were recited at the same time as the sacrifices were previously offered.

The Early-Evening Sacrifice was always offered two-and-a-half hours before nightfall, and this is therefore the most preferred time for the commencement of *Minchah.* If, however, one will have no opportunity to say *Minchah* at that hour, one may recite it at any time during the afternoon. Technically, the time for *Minchah* comes to an end at one-and-a-quarter hours before nightfall, although if one is inadvertently delayed, one may pray even until sunset.

According to the *Talmud, Minchah* is the most efficacious prayer of the day, for it was during that prayer that Elijah received a response from God during his contest with the prophets of Baal on Mount Carmel.

page 157 [232]   The *Minchah* service commences with אַשְׁרֵי. This is the third time that this psalm is recited during the daily

71

prayers - a token of its paramount importance. The fact that each line commences with a succeeding letter of the *Aleph Bet* made it easy to learn, and this may have contributed to its popularity in Talmudic times.

It is worthy of note, however, that there is no line corresponding to the letter *Nun*. The *Talmud* accounts for this omission by observing that the letter *Nun* is frequently associated with downfall, being the initial letter of the verb *nafal*, to fall. The psalmist, quite naturally, recoiled from such an association. In the following line (commencing with the letter *Samech*) he compensates with an oblique reference to that idea, in the words "the Lord upholds all that *fall (hanoflim)*".

The introduction of אַשְׁרֵי also served as a tribute to those early pietists who, according to the *Talmud*, would arrive at synagogue an hour before the start of a service in order to recite psalms. Hence we commence this service also with a psalm.

page 159 [232]   The Reader recites aloud the last two lines of אַשְׁרֵי, followed by the half-*Kaddish*.

> On Fast Days, the Reader continues with וַיְהִי בִּנְסֹעַ. He turns to face the congregation and recites the line: גַּדְּלוּ לַיָי אִתִּי, וּנְרוֹמְמָה שְׁמוֹ יַחְדָּו. (See, page 61).
>
> Three people are called to the Reading of the Law on Fast Days, with the third person reading the *Haftarah*. After the *Haftarah* he recites the concluding blessings, ending: בָּרוּךְ אַתָּה יְיָ מָגֵן דָּוִד.
>
> The Reader takes the *Sefer Torah* on his right shoulder and recites יְהַלְלוּ. As he walks back to the Ark he recites audibly לְדָוִד מִזְמוֹר and וּבְנֻחֹה יֹאמַר. On returning to the *Bimah* he recites the half-*Kaddish* (*Singer's* page 159; *ArtScroll*, page 234.

72

page 161-177 [234-248]	The congregation then recites the silent *Amidah*, which the Reader then repeats. On Fast Days we recite the section עֲנֵנוּ. The worshipper inserts it silently into the שְׁמַע קוֹלֵנוּ blessing (*Singer's*, 171; *ArtScroll*, 242); the Reader recites it as an independent blessing, between רְפָאֵנוּ and רְאֵה בְעָנְיֵנוּ. On the Fast of *Av*, both the silent worshipper as well as the Reader include the section נַחֵם after the phrase: וְכִסֵּא דָוִד מְהֵרָה לְתוֹכָהּ תָּכִין.
page 171 [244]	The section אֱלֹהֵינוּ וֵאלֹהֵי אֲבוֹתֵינוּ יַעֲלֶה וְיָבֹא is inserted on the special festive days listed in the rubric.
page 175 [246] *page* 177 [246]	Note that the Priestly Blessing, in smaller print, from the line אֱלֹהֵינוּ וֵאלֹהֵי אֲבוֹתֵינוּ בָּרְכֵנוּ בַּבְּרָכָה is included only on Fast Days. On ordinary days, the Reader continues with שָׁלוֹם רָב. Also on Fast Days, instead of the usual שָׁלוֹם רָב section, we recite שִׂים שָׁלוֹם. This is because on Fast Days we always include the Priestly Blessing, אֱלֹהֵינוּ וֵאלֹהֵי אֲבוֹתֵינוּ, בָּרְכֵנוּ, which contains the phrase יָאֵר יְיָ פָּנָיו. ("May the Lord make his face to *shine*"). It was thought more appropriate, therefore, to link this with the שִׂים שָׁלוֹם section which contains a similar metaphor: בְּאוֹר פָּנֶיךָ, ("the *light* of your face").
page 177 [248]	On reaching the end of the blessing: הַמְבָרֵךְ אֶת עַמּוֹ יִשְׂרָאֵל בַּשָּׁלוֹם,
page 179-181 [250-252]	Reader and congregation lean on the left arm to recite the *Tachanun*, (see above, pages 58 to 60).
page 183 [252] *page* 185 [254]	After concluding the last line of the *Kaddish*, the Reader recites aloud the opening words of עָלֵינוּ לְשַׁבֵּחַ. He concludes by reciting aloud the last two lines, commencing וְנֶאֱמַר, וְהָיָה יְיָ לְמֶלֶךְ, after which mourners recite *Kaddish*.

73

VII

Service for Weekday Evenings
תְּפִלַת עַרְבִית לַחוֹל

The *Ma-ariv* service was the last of the three daily services to become statutory. Since the Temple ritual contained only two daily communal offerings, it was felt that these should be replaced by only two statutory services. However, the influential leader of Palestinian Jewry, Gamaliel II (80-117 CE), forced legislation through the law-making academies to make *Ma-ariv* an official synagogue service. Gamaliel probably thought that if King David saw fit to pray 'evening, morning and at noon', and Daniel to pray 'three times daily towards Jerusalem', then it was certainly a worthy enough tradition for the Jewry of his day to preserve.

The discussion regarding the status of *Ma-ariv* as an obligatory service went on for a few centuries in the Talmudic academies of Babylon; and the authoritative view in that country, by then the hub of world Jewry, inclined to regard *Ma-ariv* as merely optional. The great codifier, Maimonides, sums up the problem in this way:

> *Ma-ariv* is not obligatory in the same way as are *Shacharit* and *Minchah*; nevertheless, all Israel, in all the countries of their domicile, have adopted the custom of reciting the *Ma-ariv* service, *and they have accepted it upon themselves as an obligatory Service.*

Maimonides based his argument upon the well-known principle, *Minhag Yisrael din hu*, that Jewish customs which become widely practised, ultimately assume the authority of law.

The optional character of *Ma-ariv* is reflected, however, in three ways: first, by the fact that the law permitted it to be recited at any time throughout the night, unlike the other two daily services which have to be recited within specific, limited times of the day. Secondly, by the fact that there is no repetition of the *Amidah* by the Reader in the *Ma-ariv* service. And thirdly, that, unlike *Shacharit*, for example, we break the prescribed fusion of the concluding blessing of the *Shema* with the *Amidah* in order to recite a half-*Kaddish*. The *Kaddish* serves to indicate that the *Amidah* is merely an optional appendage, and not, as in the other services, obligatory.

Although it is preferable to commence the *Ma-ariv* service when it is already dark, a synagogue may recite it immediately following *Minchah*, in order that the public should not be burdened with having to make a third journey to synagogue in one day.

We have hitherto referred to the Evening Service by its popular name *Ma-ariv*. This is the term which appears as the heading for this service in the *ArtScroll* edition. *Singer's*, on the other hand, employs the name *Arvit* which is the one regularly employed by Sephardi Jews to designate the Evening Service, being the older term found in the Talmudic literature. The name *Ma-ariv* was introduced later, under the influence of the phrase מַעֲרִיב עֲרָבִים in the first blessing.

page 189 [256] The section commencing וְהוּא רַחוּם is recited aloud by the Reader. It is introduced into the *Ma-ariv* service as this is the only service which does not correspond to an ancient daily sacrifice. The וְהוּא רַחוּם section serves the identical purpose as the sacrifices, namely to invoke Divine forgiveness for sins.

Another suggestion is found to account for the recitation of the וְהוּא רַחוּם verses. It seems to have been an old custom, practised in a number of medieval Jewish communities, for those found guilty of various crimes or offences to be punished publicly with symbolic thirty-nine lashes. These used to be administered just before the *Ma-ariv* service. Since this punishment had the effect of totally purging every trace of the sin, they would

76

recite the וְהוּא רַחוּם verses, which refer to the restoration to sinners of the state of grace, immediately after administering the lashes, just before *Ma-ariv*.

The Reader bows while he recites aloud the phrase: בָּרְכוּ אֶת יְיָ הַמְבוֹרָךְ, and the congregation, bowing, responds with: בָּרוּךְ יְיָ הַמְבוֹרָךְ לְעוֹלָם וָעֶד, which is repeated by the Reader.

page 189-191
[256-258]
After the congregation has recited the next section, the first of the two *Shema* benedictions, the Reader concludes by reciting the section from אֵל חַי until the blessing בָּרוּךְ אַתָּה יְיָ, הַמַּעֲרִיב עֲרָבִים.

The Reader concludes the second *Shema* benediction by reciting from כִּי הֵם חַיֵּינוּ.

page 191-195
[258-260]
THE *SHEMA*

There is no obligation to wear *Tzitzit* at night time, and for that reason the *Tallit* is not worn during this service. Hence, during the recitation of the third paragraph of the *Shema* at this point, there is no gathering together or kissing of the *Tzitzit*.

page 195 [260]
As in the case of the *Shema* recited during *Shacharit*, the *Ma-ariv Shema* is followed by a benediction depicting the redemption from Egypt. This blessing, with its expression of profound gratitude for the providence of God, has been a source of inspiration and encouragement to Jewry throughout the bitter vicissitudes of her history.

The version of this benediction recited at night commences with the word וֶאֱמוּנָה, ('and faithful'). The *Talmud* suggests that an association of ideas is intended between the use of this word and the psalm verse, "to declare your loving-kindness in the morning, and your

77

faithfulness (אֱמוּנָתֶךָ) *at night"* When the Jewish experience is as dark as night, that is when all our resources of faith and faithfulness are needed.

page 195 [262]   The Reader recites aloud commencing with the words וְאָמְרוּ כֻלָּם until וּמַלְכוּתוֹ בְּרָצוֹן קִבְּלוּ עֲלֵיהֶם. He then waits until the congregation has said the next two lines, which he repeats. The same procedure is followed for the following two lines; the Reader repeats up to זֶה אֵלִי, and completes the blessing after the congregation.

page 197 [262]   The הַשְׁכִּיבֵנוּ constitutes the second concluding blessing of the *Shema.* Its opening sentence is a request for a peaceful night of sleep followed by a renewal of life. The author develops his theme by viewing the new day not only as a personal renewal of life, but as the symbolic dawn of a new era in which the entire people of Israel is to be sheltered beneath the 'tabernacle of peace'.

page 197 [264]   The Reader recites aloud the final two lines of the blessing, from וּשְׁמוֹר צֵאתֵנוּ.

The blessing commencing בָּרוּךְ יְיָ לְעוֹלָם, אָמֵן וְאָמֵן poses a number of problems; the most serious is the fact that it seems to be in conflict with a clear statement in the *Mishnah* that at night only *two* blessings are recited after the *Shema.* This third blessing is, consequently, not even referred to by the sages of the *Talmud.* For this reason, many great halachic authorities throughout the ages refused to recite it, a view followed to this day by Sephardim.

One suggestion offered to account for its introduction is that it originated at a time of persecution when Jews could not assemble for any length of time at night. An abbreviated substitute for the *Amidah* was therefore sought; hence the introduction of this blessing, in which the Divine name occurs eighteen times, corresponding to the original eighteen blessings of the *Amidah.* Once introduced, it assumed official status, and retained its place even after the persecution had ended.

page 199 [266]   The Reader recites aloud the last four lines of the blessing, from כִּי הַמַּלְכוּת שֶׁלְּךָ הִיא, after which he recites the half-*Kaddish*. Congregation and Reader then recite the silent *Amidah*.

The Reader does not repeat the *Ma-ariv Amidah*. It is customary to wait until the Rabbi has finished saying the silent *Amidah* before reciting the full-*Kaddish* (page 215 [278]). During the period between *Pesach* and *Shavuot*, the *Omer* is counted after *Kaddish*, (page 697 [282]).

page 217 [280]   *Aleinu* is then recited, followed by the Mourner's *Kaddish*. During the whole month of *Ellul* and up to *Sh'miniy Atzeret*, psalm 27 is added, (page 145 [282]). On *Chanukah*, psalm 30 is included, (page 33 [54]).

In a house of mourning, the Rabbi recites the appropriate prayers (page 819 [174]). *ArtScroll* is remiss in not providing a full and clearly set-out service for the house of mourning, as does *Singer's* (pages 819-825).

The reason why on days of joy, when *Tachanun* is omitted, we substitute psalm 16 for psalm 49, is because, whereas the latter contains some sentiments which breathe despair regarding the human condition, as well as condemnation of man's crass materialism, psalm 16, by contrast, exudes faith, joy and confidence - sentiments far more appropriate to festive occasions.

VIII

Service for the Welcoming of Shabbat
קַבָּלַת שַׁבָּת

In winter months, the Friday Evening Service usually begins around the time of the commencement of *Shabbat.* In order to demonstrate our eagerness to celebrate *Shabbat,* and at the same time to safeguard against its accidental violation, through uncertainty as to the exact time of its commencement, we usher it in at least twenty minutes before sunset. In summer, most congregations standardize the time for *Shabbat,* around 8pm. Times for the commencement of *Shabbat* are published in the Jewish Press.

The service commences with the weekday *Minchah,* (see above, page 71), *Tachanun* being omitted. Mourners, during the week of *Shivah,* retire to the vestibule of the synagogue immediately after *Minchah.* They are called back to receive the consolation of the congregation, just before מִזְמוֹר שִׁיר לְיוֹם הַשַּׁבָּת, (see below, page 84).

 The Friday Evening Service is divided into two sections: the first is *Kabbalat Shabbat,* 'Welcoming of *Shabbat*' and is omitted when *Shabbat* coincides with, or follows immediately after, a festival. In such a case the Service commences with מִזְמוֹר שִׁיר לְיוֹם הַשַּׁבָּת. The *Kabbalat Shabbat* section comprises seven psalms, corresponding to the seven days of the week, and the poetic composition *L'chah Dodiy.* This is followed by the statutory *Ma-ariv* service, slightly modified to include *Shabbat* themes.

The *Kabbalat Shabbat* section is one of the latest additions to the Hebrew Prayer Book, having been introduced by a circle of famous mystics who lived in Safed during the 16th century. They observed many colourful ritual practices, a number of which were introduced into our own tradition. On Friday evenings they used to go out into the fields to welcome the *Shabbat* bride with joy and song. The famous mystic, Rabbi Isaac Luria, and his disciples used to recite psalm 29 as well as the *Lechah Dodiy* of Solomon Alkabetz, a leading mystical poet of that school. The Luria Synagogue remains a popular place of pilgrimage and tourist attraction in modern Israel.

Another circle of mystics expanded upon this ceremony by reciting psalms 95 - 99. The choice of these particular psalms was inspired by the Midrashic tradition that psalms 90 - 100 were composed by Moses. Since the *Torah* was given on the Sabbath, and since Moses was the intermediary for the revelation of the *Torah*, it was considered appropriate to recite his psalms on the Sabbath day.

page 223 [308]   The *Chazan* commences לְכוּ נְרַנְּנָה, and sings the conclusion of the psalm, from the phrase אַרְבָּעִים שָׁנָה.

page 225 [310]   The *Chazan* concludes psalm 96 by singing aloud from יִשְׂמְחוּ הַשָּׁמַיִם.

The *Chazan* concludes psalm 97 by singing aloud from אֹהֲבֵי יְיָ שִׂנְאוּ רָע.

page 227 [312]   The *Chazan* concludes psalm 98 by singing aloud from נְהָרוֹת יִמְחֲאוּ כָף.

The *Chazan* concludes psalm 99 by singing aloud from בְּעַמּוּד עָנָן יְדַבֵּר.

page 227 [314]   The congregation stands for the singing of the much-loved הָבוּ לַיְיָ בְּנֵי אֵלִים (psalm 29). This psalm repeats the Divine name eighteen times, a number which corresponds to the eighteen blessings in the original formulation of the *Amidah*. Just as we stand for the *Amidah*, so we stand for this psalm.

82

The inclusion of psalm 29 was primarily on account of its association with the giving of the *Torah*. The manifestation of the Divine power which, according to this psalm, made the whole of nature quake with awe, as well the references to the voice of God breaking the cedars, all refer to the mighty experience of the Revelation of God and the *Torah* on Mount Sinai. Since, according to tradition, the Revelation took place on the Sabbath, this psalm was the first choice of the mystics. The fact that the Israelites all stood up to receive the *Torah* provides an additional reason for standing during the recitation of this psalm.

page 229 [314] The *Chazan* concludes psalm 29 by singing aloud from קוֹל יְיָ יְחוֹלֵל אַיָּלוֹת.

After the concluding words of psalm 29, most synagogues recite a short composition, commencing: אָנָּא בְּכֹחַ. It is charged with mystical allusions and is supposed to contain, in secret combination, the Divine name of forty-two letters developed by the mystics as part of their system of cosmology. This composition is not included at this point in the *Singer's Prayer Book*, but is on page 703. It is recited in an undertone, and is not concluded aloud by the *Chazan* in the usual fashion.

The לְכָה דוֹדִי has been described as "perhaps one of the finest pieces of religious poetry in existence" (Solomon Schechter). Its author, Solomon Alkabetz, was born in Salonica in 1505, and settled in Safed about the year 1535. He felt the bitterness of the Jewish exile from the Holy Land to the depth of his being; and in the לְכָה דוֹדִי he gives expression to the oppressive burden of the exile ("Long enough hast though dwelt in the valley of weeping"), and the longing and passionate desire for redemption.

Each stanza begins with a succeeding letter of the poet's Hebrew name, forming the acrostic: שׁ ל מ ה ה ל ו י, Solomon the Levite. Each stanza is repeated by the

Service for the Welcoming of Shabbat

Reader, after which the congregation joins in with the refrain: לְכָה דוֹדִי לִקְרַאת כַּלָּה. פְּנֵי שַׁבָּת נְקַבְּלָה.

page 233[318] On reaching the last stanza, commencing בּוֹאִי בְשָׁלוֹם, the congregation stands and faces the back wall of the synagogue. Many fanciful explanations are offered for this, but its origin probably lies in the practice of the Cabbalists of Safed who, we are told, would face the West in order to greet the arrival of the *Shabbat* bride. The West was believed by the *Talmud* to be the direction wherein the Divine Presence dwells. Hence, since the Ark is situated against the Eastern wall of the synagogue, we turn around to face the opposite direction to recite the last stanza of the poem which contains a joyful welcome, בּוֹאִי כַלָּה, בּוֹאִי כַלָּה, "Come, O bride; Come, O bride". Where there are no mourners to greet, the service

page 233 [320] proceeds with מִזְמוֹר שִׁיר לְיוֹם הַשַּׁבָּת (psalm 92).

The recitation of psalm 92 effectively marks the onset of *Shabbat* for all present in synagogue. (The lighting of the candles brings in *Shabbat* for those at home.) Because public manifestations of mourning are prohibited on *Shabbat*, the mourners are formally welcomed and greeted by the congregation at this point in the day, immediately *before* it becomes *Shabbat* at the recitation of psalm 92.

page 235 [320] In most synagogues, psalm 93, יהוה מָלָךְ, is recited together with the previous psalm; and the *Chazan* concludes them both by reciting from מִקֹּלוֹת מַיִם רַבִּים until לְאֹרֶךְ יָמִים, after which the mourners recite *Kaddish.* Some communities recite the *Mishnah, Bameh Madlikin* at this point. Others recite it later, after *Magen Avoht* (See page 85). After *Bameh Madlikin, Kaddish d'Rabbanan* is recited (see page 39).

84

IX

Service for Shabbat Evening
עַרְבִית לְשַׁבָּת

The Evening Service for *Shabbat* is almost identical (with some additions) to that for weekdays, except that the *Chazan* sings it to a special melody. There is also a special *Shabbat* conclusion to the second (*Hashkiveinu*) blessing following the *Shema*. Instead of the weekday version. בָּרוּךְ אַתָּה יְיָ. שׁוֹמֵר עַמּוֹ יִשְׂרָאֵל לָעַד ("Who guardest Thy people, Israel, for ever"), we have a more expanded and poetic form:

הַפּוֹרֵשׂ סֻכַּת שָׁלוֹם עָלֵינוּ
וְעַל כָּל עַמּוֹ יִשְׂרָאֵל וְעַל יְרוּשָׁלָיִם

("Who spreadest the tabernacle of peace over us and over all Thy people, Israel, and over Jerusalem".).

page 247 [336]   The congregation stands for the recitation of the section commencing וְשָׁמְרוּ which is repeated by the *Chazan*. On festivals, the relevant additional verse: וַיְדַבֵּר מֹשֶׁה (Leviticus 23: 44) is added.

page 257 [346]   The *Chazan* recites the half-*Kaddish*, after which the congregation recites the silent *Amidah*. Then the *Chazan* announces the section וַיְכֻלּוּ הַשָּׁמַיִם וְהָאָרֶץ וְכָל צְבָאָם, which is chanted by the congregation and *Chazan*, still in a standing position. The *Chazan* continues with the blessing which will be recognized as almost identical - apart from the last three words - to the first blessing of the *Amidah*. After קֹנֵה שָׁמַיִם וָאָרֶץ, the congregation recites the paragraph commencing מָגֵן אָבוֹת בִּדְבָרוֹ. This section replaces the repetition of the *Amidah*, and is, in fact, phrased in such a way as to constitute an abbreviated version of the seven blessings which comprise the silent *Shabbat Amidah*, just recited. The correspondence in phraseology is worth noting:

85

Phraseology of the *Magein Avot* composition	Corresponding Phrases of the *Amidah* Blessings	Blessing Number
מָגֵן אָבוֹת ◄- - - - - - - - -	(בָּרוּךְ אַתָּה יְיָ) מָגֵן אַבְרָהָם	1
מְחַיֶּה מֵתִים ◄- - - - - - -	(בָּרוּךְ אַתָּה יְיָ) מְחַיֵּה הַמֵּתִים	2
הָאֵל הַקָּדוֹשׁ ◄- - - - - - -	(בָּרוּךְ אַתָּה יְיָ) הָאֵל הַקָּדוֹשׁ	3
הַמֵּנִיחַ לְעַמּוֹ כִּי בָם רָצָה ◄- - - - - - ◄- - - - - - - - - - - - - ﹂	רְצֵה בִמְנוּחָתֵנוּ	4
(לְפָנָיו) נַעֲבוֹד בְּיִרְאָה ◄- - - - - - -	(בָּרוּךְ אַתָּה יְיָ שֶׁאוֹתְךָ לְבַדְּךָ) בְּיִרְאָה נַעֲבוֹד:	5
וְנוֹדֶה לִשְׁמוֹ בְּכָל יוֹם ◄- - - - - ◄- - -	מוֹדִים (אֲנַחְנוּ לָךְ) (וְעַל נִסֶּיךָ) שֶׁבְּכָל יוֹם	6
מֵעֵין הַבְּרָכוֹת. ◄- - - - - - - - אֲדוֹן הַשָּׁלוֹם ◄- - - - - - - -	(בָּרוּךְ אַתָּה יְיָ) מְעוֹן הַבְּרָכוֹת וַאֲדוֹן הַשָּׁלוֹם	7

It will be noticed that the formulae of the *Amidah* blessings numbers 5 and 7 are not those that we are familiar with from our *Amidah*. They are, in fact, the original formulae as recited in ancient Israel, and the *Magein Avot* - also produced in Israel - assumes that version. Our version is the one adopted in Babylon, though we also bring back the formula of blessing No. 5 on festivals, for nationalistic and nostalgic reasons.

After the *Chazan* has repeated the מָגֵן אָבוֹת paragraph, he continues with אֱלֹהֵינוּ וֵאלֹהֵי אֲבוֹתֵינוּ, which has already been recited by the congregation during the course of the silent *Amidah*.

page 259 [348]   The *Chazan* recites the full-*Kaddish*, after which the congregation sits to recite silently the בַּמֶּה מַדְלִיקִין. This chapter of *Mishnah*, which describes the materials permitted to be used for the *Shabbat* lights, was introduced into the liturgy during the 9th century CE, as a demonstration against the view of the sectarian Karaites who maintained that it was a desecration of *Shabbat* to have lights burning on the holy day. To emphasize how misguided was this view, the Rabbis introduced into the service that very section of the *Mishnah* which describes the type of oil and wicks which may be used. There is no suggestion at all in the *Mishnah* that one may not have lights burning; the consideration is only that the specially sanctioned materials should be used. (As we have observed, some congregations recite *Bameh Madlikin* earlier in the service, as followed by ArtScroll [page 322])

After the *Chazan* has recited the concluding sentence יְיָ עֹז לְעַמּוֹ יִתֵּן יְיָ יְבָרֵךְ אֶת עַמּוֹ בַשָּׁלוֹם, the mourners recite the *Kaddish d'Rabbanan* (see page 39).

page 265 [348]   It is customary for children to ascend the *Bimah* at this point, and to remain there until the *Chazan* has concluded the *Kiddush*, after which they are given some of the wine to drink.

Between *Pesach* and *Shavuot*, the Counting of the *Omer* is performed after *Kiddush*.

page 267   The *Chazan* recites aloud the last few lines of the *Aleinu*,

87

[350-352]   from וְנֶאֱמַר, וְהָיָה, after which the mourners recite their ordinary Mourner's *Kaddish.*

During the month of *Ellul,* and until *Sh'miniy Atzeret,* psalm 27 is recited at this point, after which the mourners recite their ordinary Mourner's *Kaddish.*

page 269 [12]   The service concludes with the Reader and congregation reciting alternate lines of יִגְדַּל. *ArtScroll* follows another tradition, of reciting אֲדוֹן עוֹלָם (page 352) instead.

At the conclusion of the service one greets one's neighbour with the traditional greeting: *Shabbat Shalom,* a 'peaceful *Shabbat'.*

X

Service for Shabbat Morning
תְּפִלַּת שַׁחֲרִית לְשַׁבָּת

The *Shabbat* morning service has three main divisions:

a)   *Shacharit*

b)   *K'riat ha-Torah*

c)   *Musaf*

page 287 [368]   The first part of the service, *Shacharit*, is as for weekdays (follow the rubrics at top of page), with the addition of a number of psalms, compositions and a special *Shabbat Amidah*. We have already described the weekday *Shacharit* service in detail. We shall confine ourselves now to the various additions that are made on *Shabbat*.

page 295 [374]   Psalm 19 is a most appropriate composition with which to commence the *Shabbat* additions. "The heavens recount the glory of God, and the firmament declareth His handiwork". This aptly sums up the liturgical basis of the institution of the *Shabbat*, as a day of praise and tribute to the supreme Architect of Creation. No less creative is the *Torah*: the intellectual, moral and spiritual inspiration of the Jew. The second theme of this psalm pays tribute to the *Torah*'s unique ability to "restore the soul", "make wise the simple" and "enlighten the eyes". The Reader recites the last verse of the psalm:

יִהְיוּ לְרָצוֹן אִמְרֵי פִי, וְהֶגְיוֹן לִבִּי לְפָנֶיךָ, יְיָ צוּרִי וְגוֹאֲלִי.

page 295 [376]   The verses of psalm 34 are arranged alphabetically, though a verse commencing with letter *Vav* is omitted. Perhaps by way of compensation, an additional line was added at the end. The psalm offers sound advice to the man who wishes to lead a peaceful, long and happy life.

The psalm-heading refers to an episode in the life of David during the period when he was being pursued by the men of King Saul. David fled to the Philistine city of Gath, where he was immediately recognised, arrested and brought before the king. Fearful for his life, David feigned madness ("changed his behaviour") scraping on the doors and letting his spittle run down his beard. The king drove him out of his presence and he was able to depart in peace. The Reader recites the final line of the psalm: פּוֹדֶה יְיָ נֶפֶשׁ עֲבָדָיו, וְלֹא יֶאְשְׁמוּ כָּל הַחֹסִים בּוֹ.

page 297 [378] Psalm 90 is headed תְּפִלָּה לְמֹשֶׁה, 'A Prayer of Moses'. Although King David is traditionally credited with the authorship of the Book of Psalms, it is a composite work. The names of a number of other authors are preserved in the psalm-headings. The *Talmud* credits Moses with the authorship of psalms 90 to 100. During the *Kabbalat Shabbat* service we recite seven of Moses' psalms, and at this stage we add a few more.

page 299 [380] The Reader concludes with:

וִיהִי נֹעַם אֲדֹנָי אֱלֹהֵינוּ עָלֵינוּ,
וּמַעֲשֵׂה יָדֵינוּ כּוֹנְנָה עָלֵינוּ,
וּמַעֲשֵׂה יָדֵינוּ כּוֹנְנֵהוּ.

Psalm 91 exudes faith and confidence in the protective embrace of God that is the reward of the righteous. Although on the individual level, the self-confidence of the righteous and his immunity from persecution and destruction, as asserted by the psalmist, are not borne out by the experiences of life, yet on the national level the survival of our people, and its re-emergence in our time as a nation of consequence in its historic homeland, bears eloquent testimony to the psalmist's faith.

page 301 [382] The Reader concludes with the last verse of psalm 91:

אֹרֶךְ יָמִים אַשְׂבִּיעֵהוּ, וְאַרְאֵהוּ בִּישׁוּעָתִי,

which is repeated.

90

Psalm 135 develops the theme of the previous psalm, giving examples of the protective hand of God guiding the destiny of the nation through the successive periods of Egyptian slavery, Exodus and conquest of Canaan. The Reader concludes with the last two verses, commencing בֵּית הַלֵּוִי בָּרְכוּ אֶת יְיָ.

page 303 [384]   Psalm 136 is called 'The Great *Hallel*'. It was sung every morning and evening by the Levites of the First Temple while the Perpetual Offerings were being made. It is probable that the Levites chanted the main verses and the assembly sang the refrain כִּי לְעוֹלָם חַסְדּוֹ. It is not recited, however, in this way in the synagogue.

page 305 [386]   The Reader concludes with the last two verses, and leads straight into the first verse of the next psalm (33), as if it were the concluding verse of the previous section:

נוֹתֵן לֶחֶם לְכָל בָּשָׂר   כִּי לְעוֹלָם חַסְדּוֹ
הוֹדוּ לְאֵל הַשָּׁמָיִם   כִּי לְעוֹלָם חַסְדּוֹ
רַנְּנוּ צַדִּיקִים בַּיהוה לַיְשָׁרִים נָאוָה תְהִלָּה

The Reader ends with the last two verses of psalm 33:

כִּי בוֹ יִשְׂמַח לִבֵּנוּ, כִּי בְשֵׁם קָדְשׁוֹ בָטָחְנוּ: יְהִי חַסְדְּךָ יְיָ
עָלֵינוּ, כַּאֲשֶׁר יִחַלְנוּ לָךְ:

page 307 [388]   Psalm 92 is the principal psalm for *Shabbat*. It commences with the sentiment that, "It is a good thing to give thanks to the Lord and to sing praises". This is especially appropriate to *Shabbat* when people have the leisure and the stimulus to devote extra time to Prayer. This being one of the Moses' psalms, there is an allusion to him which can be noted in the initial letters of the heading: מִזְמוֹר שִׁיר לְיוֹם הַשַּׁבָּת, which is an anagram of the word: לְ מ שֶׁ ה, 'for Moses'.

The Reader recites the last two verses of the psalm:

עוֹד יְנוּבוּן בְּשֵׂיבָה, דְּשֵׁנִים וְרַעֲנַנִּים יִהְיוּ:
לְהַגִּיד כִּי יָשָׁר יְיָ, צוּרִי וְלֹא עַוְלָתָה בּוֹ:

The association of the following psalm (יהוה מָלָךְ) with *Shabbat* was inspired by a symbolic interpretation of the opening two verses. The Lord "robing himself in majesty" after ensuring that "the world was also set firm" symbolizes the Sabbath day which climaxed the six days of Creation. The Reader recites aloud the last verse of psalm 93:

עֵדֹתֶיךָ נֶאֶמְנוּ מְאֹד לְבֵיתְךָ נָאֲוָה קֹדֶשׁ, יהוה, לְאֹרֶךְ יָמִים.

> From this point, until the end of the Song of the Red Sea, the service follows the order of the weekday morning service (see above, pages 41 to 45), after which the *Shabbat* service continues with נִשְׁמַת.

page 323 [400] Since *Shabbat* is the occasion for extra praise of God for the benefits of Creation, the נִשְׁמַת composition gives expression to the unique power, as well as the tender mercy, of the Creator. In words of great beauty, it acknowledges the patent inability of man to assess, describe or even pay tribute to, the greatness of God:

> "Were our mouths filled with song as the sea is with water, and our tongues flowed with Prayer like perennial waves; were our lips full of praise as the wide-extended skies and our eyes beamed forth light like the sun or the moon; were our hands out-spread as the eagles of the sky, and our feet as swift as the hind - we should still be unable to thank Thee and bless Thy name..."

The נִשְׁמַת prayer is a very old composition. The *Talmud* refers to a section of the composition which originally served as a thanksgiving prayer for rain. It is also referred to by the name *Birkat ha-Shir*, 'Blessing over the Song', an allusion to its role in the *Pesach Haggadah* where it concludes the main part of the service. The term 'Blessing over the Song' may possibly refer to the morning psalms which it also concludes.

age 325 [402]   The Reader ends נִשְׁמַת by reciting the last three lines:

הָאֵל בְּתַעֲצֻמוֹת עֻזֶּךָ, הַגָּדוֹל בִּכְבוֹד שְׁמֶךָ.
הַגִּבּוֹר לָנֶצַח וְהַנּוֹרָא בְּנוֹרְאוֹתֶיךָ.
הַמֶּלֶךְ הַיּוֹשֵׁב עַל כִּסֵּא רָם וְנִשָּׂא:

after which the official synagogue *Chazan* takes over the leadership of the service.

page 325 [404]   The *Chazan* announces the phrase:

שׁוֹכֵן עַד, מָרוֹם וְקָדוֹשׁ שְׁמוֹ:.

After the congregation has recited the next paragraph, it is repeated by the *Chazan.* In many prayer books (such as *ArtScroll*) the paragraph is printed in four lines, with three words to a line, so as to highlight the name יצחק (Isaac), formed from the initial letters of the middle word of each line, thus:

תִּתְהַלָּל.	יְשָׁרִים	בְּפִי
תִּתְבָּרַךְ.	צַדִּיקִים	וּבְדִבְרֵי
תִּתְרוֹמָם.	חֲסִידִים	וּבִלְשׁוֹן
תִּתְקַדָּשׁ:	קְדוֹשִׁים	וּבְקֶרֶב

"Such fanciful ideas were, and still are, appreciated by many, whose affectionate ingenuity would play in childlike rapture round the words of the beloved prayers" (Israel Abrahams).

The *Chazan* recites from the end of the next paragraph:

לְהוֹדוֹת לְהַלֵּל לְשַׁבֵּחַ לְפָאֵר לְרוֹמֵם
לְהַדֵּר לְבָרֵךְ לְעַלֵּה וּלְקַלֵּס,
עַל כָּל דִּבְרֵי שִׁירוֹת וְתִשְׁבָּחוֹת
דָּוִד בֶּן יִשַׁי עַבְדְּךָ מְשִׁיחֶךָ:

page 327 [404]   The next paragraph, commencing יִשְׁתַּבַּח, is the same as for weekdays.

93

page 329 [408] Parts of the הַכֹּל יוֹדוּךָ composition are identical with the weekday form, which commences at הַמֵּאִיר לָאָרֶץ. It thanks the Almighty for opening 'the gates of the East' every day and providing us with the light and warmth of the sun by day, as well as with the moon by night.

The latter part of the composition, which constitutes an addition for *Shabbat*, refers to the three tenets of faith: in the World to Come, in the Coming of the Messiah and in the Resurrection of the Dead.

The *Chazan* sings aloud this last section embodying these three concepts:

אֵין כְּעֶרְכְּךָ יְיָ אֱלֹהֵינוּ, בָּעוֹלָם הַזֶּה,
וְאֵין זוּלָתְךָ מַלְכֵּנוּ לְחַיֵּי הָעוֹלָם הַבָּא.
אֶפֶס בִּלְתְּךָ גּוֹאֲלֵנוּ לִימוֹת הַמָּשִׁיחַ.
וְאֵין דּוֹמֶה לְךָ מוֹשִׁיעֵנוּ לִתְחִיַּת הַמֵּתִים:

page 331 [410] The אֵל אָדוֹן is an alphabetical hymn, continuing the theme of the previous section, though in a more mystical vein. The previous paragraph had commenced with the assertion that הַכֹּל יוֹדוּךָ ('All beings shall thank Thee'); this section demonstrates that such praise of God is not restricted to mortals, but that the whole complexity of the universe, performing with awe the will of its Master, is the greatest tribute to Him, and that in the rhythm of its unity and regularity one may discover the music of praise.

This composition clearly emanates from a circle of mystics, though the name of its author has not been preserved. The hallmark of such writers was their preoccupation with the 'celestial chariot', called *Merkavah*. They derived their inspiration from the writings of the Prophet Ezekiel who describes the heavenly court and the majestic journey of the Divine Chariot, pulled by the holy beasts (*Chayyot*), symbolic of the ever-active Divine supervision of all mankind.

P. Bloch attributes authorship of the passage to the 9th century mystical sect known as the *Yordey Merkavah*, the 'Chariot-Riders', while other scholars have suggested a greater antiquity for it, believing it to have emanated from Essene circles of the 1st century CE.

The אֵל אָדוֹן stanzas are either chanted alternately by *Chazan* and congregation or sung as a congregational hymn.

The *Chazan* announces the opening words of the following paragraph:

לָאֵל אֲשֶׁר שָׁבַת מִכָּל הַמַּעֲשִׂים,

and the congregation recites this together with the succeeding paragraph, תִּתְבָּרַךְ צוּרֵנוּ, without pausing.

pages 333-349 [412-420]

These pages are identical with the weekday morning service version (see above, pages 48 to 53).

pages 347 [422]

This *Kedushah* is an expanded form of the one recited during the repetition of the weekday *Amidah*. The basis of the *Kedushah* is the formula used by the heavenly spirits to praise God. This formula is disclosed by Isaiah in his majestic description of heaven:

וְקָרָא זֶה אֶל זֶה וְאָמַר:
קָדוֹשׁ קָדוֹשׁ קָדוֹשׁ יְיָ צְבָאוֹת,
מְלֹא כָל הָאָרֶץ כְּבוֹדוֹ.

And they called, one unto the other, and said:
"Holy, Holy, Holy is the Lord of hosts:
the whole earth is full of His glory".

The Prophet Ezekiel had a similar celestial disclosure; and the formula he reports constitutes the second source of the *Kedushah*:

And a wind lifted me up, and I heard behind me a noise of great rushing (קוֹל רַעַשׁ גָּדוֹל);

95

"Blessed be the glory of the Lord from his place"

(בָּרוּךְ כְּבוֹד יְיָ, מִמְּקוֹמוֹ).

The section from אָז בְּקוֹל רַעַשׁ גָּדוֹל, which is added in the *Shabbat Kedushah*, is thus derived from the Ezekiel formula. The last paragraph, מִמְּקוֹמְךָ מַלְכֵּנוּ תוֹפִיעַ, looks forward to a restoration, in Jerusalem, of Divine rule.

pages 349-351
[424]

The four paragraphs which follow combine to constitute the intermediate blessing of the *Shabbat Amidah*.

The יִשְׂמַח מֹשֶׁה paragraph describes the great joy felt by Moses as he presented Israel with the *Shabbat* law, engraved upon the two tablets of stone.

It is noteworthy that, instead of proceeding to quote the fourth commandment, as expected from the context, the *Siddur* uses a totally different scriptural passage, namely וְשָׁמְרוּ (Exodus 31: 16-17). This omission of a quotation from the Ten Commandments is intentional. In Temple times the Ten Commandments were an intrinsic part of the daily services. However, when the early Christians rejected the authority of the whole *Torah*, accepting only the Ten Commandments as the word of God, the Rabbis withdrew it from the liturgy in order not to invest it with too much emphasis at the expense of the rest of the 613 commandments of the *Torah*.

The author of the וְלֹא נְתַתּוֹ section emphasizes that *Shabbat* was intended as a special boon to Israel, a token of love for those who were prepared to hallow it. The reference to "the uncircumcised who do not dwell in it" might be directed at Christianity which, while accepting the Sabbath, rejected most of the other laws of the *Torah*.

page 351 [424]

The section commencing אֱלֹהֵינוּ, וֵאלֹהֵי אֲבוֹתֵינוּ serves as the conclusion of the *Shabbat* intermediate blessing in each of the four *Amidahs* recited on this day.

page 357 [430]   After the *Chazan* has concluded his repetition of the *Amidah,* he recites the full-*Kaddish.* On festivals and *Rosh Chodesh* he commences *Hallel* immediately after the concluding words of the *Amidah:*

הַמְבָרֵךְ אֶת עַמּוֹ יִשְׂרָאֵל בַּשָּׁלוֹם.

סֵדֶר קְרִיאַת הַתּוֹרָה לְשַׁבָּת וְיוֹם טוֹב

THE ORDER OF THE READING OF THE LAW

page 361 [432]   The congregation remains standing, after the *Kaddish,* for the chanting of אֵין כָּמוֹךְ. The one who has been honoured with *P'tichah* - the opening of the Ark - walks towards the Ark as the *Chazan* commences אֵין כָּמוֹךְ. He opens the Ark after the phrase רָם וְנִשָּׂא אֲדוֹן עוֹלָמִים. He then stands next to the open Ark while the *Chazan* and congregation sing וַיְהִי בִּנְסוֹעַ. After singing the line:

בָּרוּךְ שֶׁנָּתַן תּוֹרָה לְעַמּוֹ יִשְׂרָאֵל בִּקְדֻשָּׁתוֹ,

the congregation recites the בְּרִיךְ שְׁמֵהּ paragraph silently, until לְטַב וּלְחַיִּין וְלִשְׁלָם. The one who has *P'tichah* then hands the *Sefer Torah* to the *Chazan.*

pages 361-363 [434]   On festivals, he waits before taking out the *Sefer Torah* until the verse יְיָ, יְיָ, אֵל רַחוּם וְחַנּוּן, has been sung three times, the section from רִבּוֹן הָעוֹלָם has been recited and the verse וַאֲנִי תְפִלָּתִי has been sung three times..

The *Chazan,* and those standing with him in front of the Ark, turn to face the congregation. They sing, alternately, the three verses:

שְׁמַע יִשְׂרָאֵל, יְיָ אֱלֹהֵינוּ, יְיָ אֶחָד.
אֶחָד אֱלֹהֵינוּ, גָּדוֹל אֲדוֹנֵנוּ, קָדוֹשׁ שְׁמוֹ.
גַּדְּלוּ לַיְיָ אִתִּי, וּנְרוֹמְמָה שְׁמוֹ יַחְדָּו.

As the *Chazan* steps away from the Ark, to make his way towards the *Bimah*, the one who has *P'tichah* closes the Ark and takes up the rear of the procession. As the procession ascends the steps of the *Bimah*, he returns to his own place.

THE READING OF THE LAW AND *HAFTARAH*

A considerable development has taken place in the manner in which the Reading of the Law has been conducted since Talmudic times. Originally, the person 'called up' for an *Aliyah* had to read his own portion from the *Torah*. Anyone unable to do so was not called up. In a synagogue where there were not seven people capable of acting as *Ba-al K'riah* (Public Reader) on *Shabbat* morning, those capable were called up again, as often as required.

It was the famous Saadia Gaon, (10th century), who made the first concession to ignorance by permitting the *Chazan* to prompt an ignorant *Cohen* in the reading where there was no other *Cohen* present to be called up. By the 12th century it had become the established custom for the *Chazan* to act as general prompter, and this was but one step away from that official taking over completely the reading of the *Torah*, to enable any worshipper to be called up.

Another feature of the original practice of the reading of the *Torah* was for the first one called up (only) to recite the opening blessing, and the last one (only) to recite the concluding blessing.

The Miy Shebeirach

After the *Ba-al K'riah* has read a *Parashah*, and the one called up has recited the concluding blessing, a *Miy Shebeirach* blessing is recited by the *Ba-al K'riah* or a Warden. (see *Singer's*, pages 913-917; *ArtScroll*, pages

442-443a). In this petition he mentions the Hebrew name of the one called up, and specifies the close members of his family, calling upon the Almighty to grant them all happiness, blessing and prosperity, "together with all Israel their brethren".

On *Shabbat* and festivals many congregations maintain the practice of inviting those called up to make a donation to charity or to the synagogue, and include a reference to that generous act into the formula of the *Miy Shebeirach*. The act of charity, it is believed, would assure the fulfilment of the blessings petitioned for. One can, of course, donate as much or as little as one wishes. If one does not wish to specify publicly the amount of one's donation, one simply instructs the Warden to include the word *matanah*, 'a gift'.

A member who has *Yahrzeit* during the following week is a priority for an *Aliyah*. A special *Hazkarah*, memorial Prayer, is recited for the repose of the departed soul. It is necessary to know the Hebrew name of the departed beforehand, since it is specified in the *Hazkarah*. A special Prayer for the sick may also be recited at this stage.

Where a baby girl has been born, the father is called up for an *Aliyah* on the first *Shabbat* after the birth, when a special *Miy Shebeirach* is recited, during which the child is given her Hebrew name. The guidance of the Rabbi should be sought beforehand regarding a suitable Hebrew name.

After the *Sidrah* has been completed, half-*Kaddish* is recited by the *Ba-al K'riah* or the *Chazan*, after which a member is called up for *Maftir*. *Maftir* means 'conclusion', and indicates the honour of concluding the weekly Scriptural reading.

On *Rosh Chodesh* and festivals there are specially prescribed *Maftirs*, which are read from a second scroll. The *Maftir* on an ordinary *Shabbat* is merely the repetition of the last few verses of the *Sidrah*. The main task of the one called up for *Maftir* is to read the section from the Prophetic Writings, called the *Haftarah*. The Talmud states that one may not read the *Haftarah* unless he has previously read a portion of the *Sidrah*; and for this reason the last few verses of the *Sidrah* are repeated for his benefit.

After the *Maftir* has been read, two people are called up for *Hagbahah* and *G'lilah* (see above, page 65). The Scroll is then lifted up and the congregation sings:

וְזֹאת הַתּוֹרָה אֲשֶׁר שָׂם מֹשֶׁה לִפְנֵי בְּנֵי יִשְׂרָאֵל
עַל פִּי יְיָ בְּיַד מֹשֶׁה:

The *Haftarah* is then sung to a special melody, a variation of the melody employed for the Reading of the *Torah*. In some congregations, the one who has performed *G'lilah*, the dressing of the Scroll, returns to his place immediately after completing his *Mitzvah*, and the one who has performed *Hagbahah* sits holding the Scroll throughout the reading of the *Haftarah* until the recitation of the Prayer for the Royal Family or the Government. He then remains standing on the *Bimah* and joins the procession which accompanies the Scroll back to the Ark. In other congregations, both the *Hagbahah* and the *G'lilah* remain on the *Bimah*.

The origin of the custom to read a *Haftarah*, is uncertain. It is generally regarded as having originated in the face of the restrictive measures imposed upon Palestinian Jewry by Antiochus Epiphanes (ca 168 BCE), including one forbidding the public reading from the *Torah*. The Jews reacted by introducing a substitute, in the form of a reading from the Prophetic Writings which, unlike the *Torah* itself, could be recited orally. The *Haftarah* they chose each week always corresponded, either in theme or spirit, to the *Sidrah* that, under normal circumstances, would have been read. After the Maccabean victory, when the practice of reading from the *Torah* was reintroduced, the custom of reciting a

Haftarah was, nevertheless, retained.

pages 373-375
[446-448] The one called up to *Maftir* and *Haftarah* recites seven blessings, corresponding to the minimum number of people called up to the Reading of the law on *Shabbat* mornings.

pages 377-379
[448-450] After the reading of the *Haftarah*, the *Chazan* announces יְקוּם פָּרְקָן, and the congregation recites the next three paragraphs

Y'kum Porkan

Our Prayers reflect the vicissitudes of Jewry over a span of nearly three thousand years, from Biblical times until the end of the Middle Ages, and even including a few modern-day compositions reflecting the contemporary situation. The Jew regards his history not as a fossil, but as a source of inspiration and pride, and an unfolding of the special destiny to which he is heir. In the light of this we explain the relevance of the יְקוּם פָּרְקָן Prayer, even though it refers to institutions and conditions far removed, in time and place, from the situation of modern Jewry. A glance at the translation will reveal that the יְקוּם פָּרְקָן is a Prayer for the health and prosperity of the spiritual, educational and judicial leaders of Babylon and Palestine. The language is not pure Hebrew, but Aramaic, reflecting the Babylonian origin of the Prayer. Among the dignitaries referred to are:

רֵישֵׁי כַלֵּי - 'The Heads of the Seminars'. These Seminars, or *Kallahs*, were twice-yearly conventions, held during the months of *Adar* (before *Pesach*) and *Ellul* (before *Rosh Hashanah)*, for scholars, teachers and laymen. As an Open University, it made a great impact upon the spiritual and cultural life of Babylonian Jewry.

רֵישֵׁי גָלְוָתָא - 'The Chiefs of the Captivity'. This refers to the position of Exilarch, the supreme leader of

Babylonian Jewry. This office had monarchic authority, due to the fact that the Exilarchs traced their ancestry back to the royal house of David. The office continued until the middle of the 11th century when Jewish life in the East waned and the centre of spiritual gravity was transferred to Europe.

רֵישֵׁי מְתִיבָתָא - 'The Principals of the Colleges'. Two colleges, situated in Sura and Pumbedita, constituted the points of focus of world Jewry from the end of the 3rd century CE, after the decline of spiritual life in Palestine caused by Roman persecution. These two Babylonian Colleges were responsible for the development of Jewish law and ritual that was ultimately recorded in the authoritative Babylonian *Talmud*.

The second paragraph of יְקוּם פָּרְקָן, almost identical in its phraseology to the first, omits references to the Babylonian institutions. It is a Prayer for the physical well-being and religious loyalty of the particular congregation to which the worshipper belongs.

Religious loyalty is the theme of the paragraph commencing מִי שֶׁבֵּרַךְ. Loyalty does not mean lip-service to an ideal; it means total and active commitment, even to the minutiae of the needs and requirements of the community or the synagogue. Nothing performed in the service of God can be considered menial or trivial. The small contributions - "lamps for lighting and wine for *Kiddush* and *Havdalah*" - if offered spontaneously and with love, weigh more in the sight of God than the munificent contributions of the rich, if offered for motives of personal vanity.

תְּפִלָּה לִשְׁלוֹם הַמַּלְכוּת
Prayer for the Royal Family or the Government

page 381 [450]   The *Sefer Torah* is brought to the desk and the congregation rises for Prayers for the Royal Family, or the President and Government, and for the State of Israel. These are recited by the Rabbi.

Throughout the long night of exile, the Jew was never found wanting in his unswerving loyalty to the country that afforded him refuge and protection. This deep-seated, natural gratitude was reinforced by a religious obligation, first enunciated by the prophet Jeremiah, to "Seek the welfare of any city to which I have carried you off, and pray to the Lord for it; on its welfare your welfare will depend".

Although it is traditional in the United States to say a Prayer for the welfare of the President, Vice-President and Governors of States, *ArtScroll* does not include such a Prayer, but merely refers to it. More unpardonable is its omission of the Prayer for the State of Israel!

תְּפִלָּה לִשְׁלוֹם מְדִינַת יִשְׂרָאֵל
Prayer for the Welfare of the State of Israel

In the previous two sections the theme of loyalty was highlighted: loyalty to our religious tradition and loyalty to the country of our domicile. Since the establishment of the State of Israel, in 1948, a further sense of loyalty is demanded of the Jew. The common ties of brotherhood that unite our people impose a special responsibility upon the Jews of the Diaspora, to ensure the survival and security of Israel by financial and moral support, and by Prayer for its welfare.

This Prayer emphasizes the religious significance of the State of Israel. For the Jew of the Diaspora, there can be no suggestion of dual-loyalty. His support of Israel does not conflict with his allegiance to the country where he resides. Israel is vital to the fulfilment of the spiritual mission of world Jewry, and to the humanitarian effort of bringing millions of our brethren from countries where they are discriminated against or in peril (such as the former Soviet Union) - a role that no other country can or will discharge. The spiritual role of the State is implied in the phrase "for out of Zion shall go forth the law and the word of the Lord from Jerusalem".

בִּרְכַּת הַחוֹדֶשׁ
Blessing of the New Month

page 383 [452] The *Shabbat* preceding each new moon is called *Shabbat M'vorachim ha-Chodesh*, 'The *Shabbat* of the Sanctification of the New Month'. The Jewish Calendar is basically lunar, consisting of twelve months, each of approximately twenty-nine-and-a-half-days, making a total of 354 days in the year. (Because we cannot commence a new month in the middle of a day, we observe six months of twenty-nine days and six months of thirty days.)

In ancient times, the new month was 'sanctified' and officially announced by a special Court that sat in Jerusalem to hear the evidence of witnesses testifying to have actually observed the appearance of the new moon the previous night. This colourful procedure was later replaced by a fixed calendar based upon astronomical calculation.

The יְהִי רָצוֹן Prayer is recited by the congregation and repeated by the *Chazan*. The waning of the old and the birth of the new moon symbolizes the spirit of optimism and faith that has enabled the Jew to view even his most desperate plight as but a passing cloud. Each month, the recitation of this Prayer gave to the sick the promise of "bodily vigour"; to those at war the hope of "a life of peace"; to the poor, the expectation of "goodness blessing and sustenance"; and to the wayward the call to "a life marked by the fear of Heaven and the dread of sin". The spirit of renewal, engendered by the new

page 385 [452] moon, reaches a climax in the מִי שֶׁעָשָׂה נִסִּים Prayer, where the messianic dawn of Israel's renewed national liberation is imminently expected.

104

The *Chazan* announces the name of the forthcoming month and the day or days of the coming week upon which it occurs. If the current month is a full one, consisting of thirty days, then two days of *Rosh Chodesh* are celebrated: the last day of the current month and the first day of the next month. When the current month is 'deficient' (ie of only twenty-nine days), then only one day of *Rosh Chodesh*, namely the first day of the new month, is celebrated.

The congregation repeats the announcement, and immediately continues with the יְחַדְּשֵׁהוּ section. After the *Chazan* has repeated this, the congregation responds with אָמֵן after each of the three phrases:

...לְחַיִּים וּלְשָׁלוֹם.

...לְשָׂשׂוֹן וּלְשִׂמְחָה.

...לִישׁוּעָה וּלְנֶחָמָה.

page 385 [454]   The אַב הָרַחֲמִים is a requiem for the martyrs of the Jewish communities of the Rhineland who were massacred during the period of the Crusades. Voices have frequently been raised objecting to the spirit of vengeance that this composition seems to breathe. The effect of this has been to confine its recitation in many congregations to the Sabbaths preceding *Shavuot* and the Fast of the Ninth of *Av*.

Shavuot was singled out since it terminates the *Sefirah* period of national mourning, and also, by a strange and bitter coincidence, since it was about the time of this festival that many of the most devastating attacks on Jewish communities were perpetrated in the Crusading era. The Ninth of *Av* is the anniversary of the destruction of the Temple, which marked the end of Jewish independence on the soil of the Holy Land, and set in motion the cycle of exile and oppression, of which the Crusades were a particularly tragic manifestation.

page 387 [456]   The *Chazan* announces the first line of אַשְׁרֵי. He sings the end of the psalm, from תְּהִלַּת יְיָ יְדַבֶּר, and the congregation joins in the singing of the last line:

וַאֲנַחְנוּ נְבָרֵךְ יָהּ, מֵעַתָּה וְעַד עוֹלָם, הַלְלוּיָהּ:

While the congregation is reciting *Ashrei*, the one who had opened the Ark previously for the taking out of the *Sefer Torah* makes his way back to the Ark. He opens it as the last line of *Ashrei* is being sung.

page 389 [458]   After the *Chazan* has recited יְהַלְלוּ, the congregation sings the section commencing הוֹדוֹ עַל אֶרֶץ וְשָׁמָיִם.

The *Chazan* announces the words מִזְמוֹר לְדָוִד, and the congregation sings psalm 29, הָבוּ לַייָ בְּנֵי אֵלִים, to a joyful and popular melody. While this psalm is being sung, the *Chazan* leads the procession from the *Bimah* to return the Scrolls to the Ark.

page 391 [460]   On festivals occurring on weekdays, לְדָוִד מִזְמוֹר is substituted for the latter psalm.

The congregation recites וּבְנֻחֹה יֹאמַר, the concluding verses of which are sung by the *Chazan*. When he reaches the last word, כְּקֶדֶם, the Ark is closed and those who have escorted the *Sefer Torah* back to the Ark return to their seats. At this point in the service the Rabbi delivers the Sermon, after which the *Chazan* recites the half-*Kaddish*, and the congregation stands, facing the Ark with feet together, to recite the silent *Amidah* which begins the *Musaf* service.

106

XI

Additional Service for Shabbat
תְּפִלַּת מוּסָף לְשַׁבָּת

page 395 [462] On *Shabbat,* as well as on *Rosh Chodesh* and festivals, we recite the *Musaf* (Additional Service), since the *Torah* prescribed additional offerings for those occasions. The *Musaf Amidah* consequently refers, almost exclusively, to the details of the additional offerings brought on that day in the desert sanctuary and, subsequently, in the Temple in Jerusalem.

While it is admitted that details of the ancient sacrificial cult are hardly likely to inspire devotion in the hearts and minds of the modern Jew, it cannot be denied, however, that the Temple idea has served as an inspirational symbol of Jewish religious unity and national cohesion throughout two thousand years of exile.

The reunification of Jerusalem in our time, and the restoration of the Western Wall to Jewish possession, can only be fully appreciated or justified when viewed as the inevitable Divine response to the prayers and aspirations of a Jewry that never tired of studying and recounting even the most abstruse details of life and ritual in its ancient spiritual capital. The recitation of the *Shabbat Musaf Amidah* was instrumental, therefore, in keeping intact the oft-overstrained spiritual and emotional life-line between the Jew, his past history, and his hopes of future redemption.

To omit the sacrificial passages of our Prayer Book is to erase from our religious and national scrapbook the priceless memories of a glorious adolescence. Even for those who consider the sacrificial cult to have been but a stage in the climb towards religious maturity, that is no reason to blot out every trace of its existence and essential contribution.

Our nation, that has been called upon in every generation to make the supreme sacrifice of the lives of its dear ones, has learnt to regard the contents of the *Musaf Amidah*, with its emphasis on sacrifice, as symbolic of our own tragic experience. The certain knowledge that our martyrs did not die in vain, but that every drop of blood constituted a sacred act of sacrifice, made our burden all the easier to bear, and provided an extra dimension to the liturgical recollection of our ancient Temple ritual.

page 397 {464} The *Chazan* repeats the *Amidah*, and the congregation stands for the *Kedushah*. The *Musaf Kedushah* is a further expansion of the one recited during *Shacharit*, so as to include a new theme, that of שְׁמַע יִשְׂרָאֵל, the Unity of God.

The insertion of the *Shema* into the *Kedushah* has been explained with reference to the persecution initiated against the Jews of Babylon by the Persian King, Jezdegaard II, about the year 455 CE. Among his attempts to curb even private religious practices, was the banning of the *Shema*, since its emphasis on God's unity was construed by the dominant Zoroastrian religion as a denial of their belief in the doctrine of the dual deity of good and evil. The Rabbis of the day were consequently forced to accede to its removal from the service. However, in order to keep alive its recitation they smuggled a reference to it into the *Kedushah* prayer. This took the form of reciting just the first line of the first paragraph and the last line of the third paragraph of the *Shema*, as part of the *Kedushah*. Presumably, this was recited rather rapidly so as to be inaudible to the ear of any Persian official who might chance to pay an unexpected visit to the synagogue to ensure that the Jews were obeying instructions.

During the period of the persecution, the *Shema* would have been indicated in this way during every *Kedushah*, both on weekdays as well as on *Shabbat*. Once the situation improved, and the decree outlawing its

108

recitation had been rescinded, the custom of including a reference to the *Shema* was abandoned in the case of every *Kedushah*, except *Musaf.* It was retained in the *Musaf Kedushah* in order to preserve a record of the deliverance from that particular persecution. The choice of *Musaf* was because the *Shema* is not prescribed for that service, and thus no unnecessary repetition is involved by including it in its *Kedushah*.

page 407 [472]
page 413 [476]
After the *Chazan* has reached the end of the *Amidah*, he recites the *Kaddish Titkabbal* (see above, page 68). The *Chazan* and congregation then sing אֵין כֵּאלֹהֵינוּ, a hymn that captures, in the simplicity of its vocabulary, the fervent joy and depth of feeling that characterizes the relationship, through worship, between Israel and God.

It has been noted that one would have expected the hymn to have begun with the second stanza מִי כֵּאלֹהֵינוּ, "Who is like our God?", and then to have followed with the logical answer, אֵין כֵּאלֹהֵינוּ, "There is none like our God". The stanzas were probably transposed so that the initial letters of the first three stanzas would make up the word אָמֵן.

The last verse, "Thou art He unto whom our fathers burnt the incense of spices", was an addition to the hymn in order to connect it with the following section which gives details of the compounds used in Temple times to make the aromatic incense. This was burnt upon an altar assigned for that purpose which was inside the *Hechal*, the chamber adjoining the Holy of Holies.

pages 413-415
[476-478]
From פִּטוּם הַקְּטֹרֶת until יְיָ יְבָרֵךְ אֶת עַמּוֹ בַשָּׁלוֹם, is recited silently. It is omitted in many congregations.

After the section dealing with the incense, there follows a second passage from Talmudic literature. From this particular *Mishnah* we derive our knowledge of the special psalms prescribed for each day of the week, הַשִּׁיר שֶׁהַלְוִיִּם הָיוּ אוֹמְרִים בְּבֵית הַמִּקְדָּשׁ. While other psalms were also recited in the Temple during the course of each day, it was the daily psalm, specified in this *Mishnah*, which brought the service to a close. It was sung *fortissimo* by the Levitical choir while the final ritual act, the offering of wine, was performed.

The final section in this collection of Talmudic passages refers to the greatest gift that mankind can be heir to - the gift of peace. It has been noted that the word for peace, שָׁלוֹם, occurs six times in the passage, thus explaining its relationship to the previous paragraph which listed the days of the week. While *Shabbat* is itself the agent of peace, it is necessary to invoke the blessing of peace upon the six working days.

The *Chazan* announces the end of the passage:

יְיָ עֹז לְעַמּוֹ יִתֵּן, יְיָ יְבָרֵךְ אֶת עַמּוֹ בַשָּׁלוֹם,

after which mourners recite the *Kaddish d'Rabbanan* (see above, page 39).

In many synagogues the above passages are omitted, and, after concluding אֵין כֵּאלֹהֵינוּ, they proceed straight to *Aleinu*.

page 415 [480]
[417-482] *Aleinu* (see above, page 68), is then followed by the Mourner's *Kaddish*.

page 419 [484] The Ark is opened for שִׁיר הַכָּבוֹד, Hymn of Glory, the verses of which are sung alternately by *Chazan* and Congregation. Both the honour of singing the Hymn and opening the Ark are frequently given to a youngster. (For transliteration, see below, page 169).

The Hymn of Glory was composed by Judah he-Chasid (the Pious), the renowned leader of a pietistic circle which flourished in Germany during the 13th and 14th centuries. A considerable amount of criticism has been levelled against the hymn, by less poetically and mystically-inspired Rabbis, on the grounds that its amorous sentiments and physical descriptions of God are unseemly, if not blasphemous. In defence of the author, it must be stated that it is a sad reflection on the cold hearts, the too-sober intellects and the stony emotions of his critics, if they could not but admire and treasure the out-pouring of a unique soul that discovered the emotional reality of God, and that fell in love with that reality.

page 423 [486]   While the congregation is singing the last line, מִי יְמַלֵּל, of the following paragraph, the Ark is closed. Some congregations recite a Mourner's *Kaddish* here, before
page 307 [488]   proceeding to the Psalm for the Sabbath Day (psalm 92), commencing מִזְמוֹר שִׁיר לְיוֹם הַשַּׁבָּת. Just as the recitation of the special psalm for the day served as the conclusion of the daily service in the Temple, so it is recited at the conclusion of each of our morning services. The *Chazan* recites the concluding verse of the psalm, לְהַגִּיד כִּי יָשָׁר יְיָ צוּרִי וְלֹא עַוְלָתָה בּוֹ, after which the Mourner's *Kaddish* is again said. During the month of *Ellul*, and through until *Sh'miniy Atzeret*, psalm 27 (לְדָוִד יְיָ אוֹרִי) is recited here.

page 423 [488]   The Service concludes with the congregational singing of
page 425 [12]   אֲדוֹן עוֹלָם, "the most popular hymn added to our liturgy since Bible times" (J.H.Hertz). The hymn expresses Judaism's affirmation of God as Creator and its uncompromising opposition to the theory of the eternity of the universe, namely that it was always there, without Divine initiation. It asserts the fundamental truth of God's existence before He assumed the role of Creator, as well as at the end of time when Creation will have served His sovereign purpose. Although He stands above Creation, transcending the physical world, God also enters into the closest relationship with man: He is man's strength "in sorrow's darkest day", and the guardian of man's soul while he sleeps. The latter theme, with which the hymn ends, has led to the suggestion that it was originally composed as a night prayer.

XII

Service for Shabbat Afternoon
תְּפִלַת מִנְחָה לְשַׁבָּת

page 439 [502] The *Shabbat* afternoon service, *Minchah,* is read approximately one hour before the termination of *Shabbat.* The service commences with אַשְׁרֵי, as on weekday afternoons. This is followed by וּבָא לְצִיּוֹן גּוֹאֵל. We have already traced the origin of the latter prayer to the study meetings that used to be held after the weekday morning services in Talmudic and early medieval times (see above page 66). *Shabbat* afternoons were also occasions for study, when the distinguished scholars would deliver public lectures (*d'rashot*), after which they prayed the Afternoon Service. As was their custom, at the conclusion of the lecture they would recite several Messianic verses, the favourite choice being וּבָא לְצִיּוֹן גּוֹאֵל. In the course of time this prayer became an integral part of the *Shabbat Minchah* service, even in communities where the latter was not preceded by a study circle.

page 443-445
[506] After the *Chazan* has sung the concluding verses:

וְיִבְטְחוּ בְךָ יוֹדְעֵי שְׁמֶךָ, כִּי לֹא עָזַבְתָּ דוֹרְשֶׁיךָ יְיָ:
יְיָ חָפֵץ לְמַעַן צִדְקוֹ, יַגְדִּיל תּוֹרָה וְיַאְדִּיר.

he recites the half-*Kaddish.* The congregation then recites the verse וַאֲנִי תְפִלָּתִי. This serves as an introduction to the next section, the Reading of the *Torah.* The phrase וַאֲנִי תְפִלָּתִי לְךָ יְיָ עֵת רָצוֹן ("And as for me, may my prayer unto Thee, O Lord, be in an acceptable time"), was explained by our sages to refer to the time when the *Sefer Torah* is read. This is the most 'acceptable time' in which to petition the Almighty. Thus, when we do not read from the *Torah* at the Afternoon Service, for example on festivals which occur on weekdays, the וַאֲנִי תְפִלָּתִי is omitted.

113

The *Chazan* adopts the same procedure as on weekday mornings for the taking out of the *Sefer Torah* from the Ark (see above, pages 61, ff). Three people are called up to the reading, which consists of the first portion of the *Sidrah* for the following week. According to the *Talmud*, the obligation of reading from the *Torah* on *Shabbat* afternoons was introduced by Ezra the Scribe for the benefit of shopkeepers who found it impossible to assemble in the market places on Monday and Thursday mornings to hear the *Torah* read. To quench their spiritual thirst, an additional reading was prescribed for *Shabbat* afternoons.

After the three people have been called up to the *Torah*, two others are called to perform *Hagbahah* and *G'lilah*. While the *Torah* is being dressed, the *Chazan* leads the congregation in the recitation of מִזְמוֹר שִׁיר לְיוֹם הַשַּׁבָּת (*Singer's* page 307; *ArtScroll*, page 488).

page 455-457
[514-522]

page 449 [516]
After the *Torah* has been returned to the Ark, the *Chazan* recites the half-*Kaddish*, after which the silent *Amidah* is said by the congregation. This is repeated by the *Chazan*, who sings it to a special melody, traditionally assigned to this service. The *Kedushah* is identical with the weekday one, and recited in the same way.

The intermediate blessing, אַתָּה אֶחָד וְשִׁמְךָ אֶחָד, highlights three unique concepts: God ("Thou art one and Thy name is one"); Israel ("And who is like Thy people Israel, a unique nation on earth"), and the *Shabbat* ("Glorious greatness and a crown of salvation, the day of rest and holiness, Thou hast given unto Thy people"). It then proceeds to stress the joy which the *Shabbat* brought to the Patriarchs, Abraham, Isaac and Jacob. The purpose of that reference was to underline the Rabbinic tradition that the Patriarchs kept the commandments even before they became binding upon Israel at Mount Sinai.

The *Chazan* concludes the repetition of the *Amidah* with

page 457 [524]

בָּרוּךְ אַתָּה יְיָ, הַמְבָרֵךְ אֶת עַמּוֹ יִשְׂרָאֵל בַּשָּׁלוֹם,

after which the congregation recites צִדְקָתְךָ צֶדֶק.

The three verses which constitute צִדְקָתְךָ צֶדֶק have as their theme the vindication of God's righteousness. Such a theme is usually associated with the demise of a person, and the burial service is, in fact, referred to by the name צִדּוּק הַדִּין ('The justification of the Divine decision'). It has been suggested, therefore, that these verses commemorate the death of Moses, who is supposed to have died on *Shabbat* at *Minchah* time. Since צִדְקָתְךָ צֶדֶק is a form of burial service, it is omitted on days which have a festive character.

The *Chazan* repeats the last verse, צִדְקָתְךָ כְּהַרְרֵי אֵל, after which he recites the full-*Kaddish*.

page 461-471 [530-542]

Throughout the Autumn and Winter months, the service continues with בָּרְכִי נַפְשִׁי (psalm 104), and the fifteen psalms, all commencing with the heading שִׁיר הַמַּעֲלוֹת.

Since we commence reading this selection on *Shabbat Bereshit*, when we read from the *Torah* the account of the Creation, בָּרְכִי נַפְשִׁי was regarded as most appropriate for that occasion, since it describes in poetic terms the first flush of Creation, the first bloom of nature and the reliance of all living things upon the sustaining grace and bounty of God.

The meaning of the psalm heading *Shir ha-Ma-alot* is uncertain. The word *Ma-alot* means, 'going up' or 'ascent'. Early commentators explained this to refer to the going up to Israel after the Babylonian exile, when the returning exiles would have composed or sung these psalms. Others refer the term to the fifteen 'steps' in the Temple, from where the Levites sang psalms.

Modern scholars fight shy from identifying any one historical situation as the background to these psalms.

115

They explain the word *Ma-alot* in terms of regular ascent, or pilgrimages, to Jerusalem for the feasts prescribed by the *Torah*. We learn from psalm 42: 5 that song, music, sacred dances and exultant shouts accompanied the processions of pilgrims. The *Shir ha-Ma-alot* psalms were probably the special favourites for these occasions as they have a common social and patriotic character and could all have been sung to the same tune.

page 471 [542]   The *Chazan* recites the final psalm, which is followed by the Mourner's *Kaddish*. The congregation then recites *Aleinu*, followed again by the Mourner's *Kaddish*.

During the summer months, from the *Shabbat* after *Pesach* until the *Shabbat* before *Rosh Hashanah*, instead of בָּרְכִי נַפְשִׁי, we read a succeeding chapter each week of פִּרְקֵי אָבוֹת, Ethics of the Fathers.

פִּרְקֵי אָבוֹת
Ethics of the Fathers

page 477-525 [544-586]   The custom of reciting *Pirkei Avot* originated around the 9th century CE, in the Babylonian academy of Sura. Its restriction to the summer months is possibly because that is the time when people are prone to pleasure and frolic, and are more in need of the moral and ethical exhortations contained in the Ethics of the Fathers.

We have referred to the fact that during that time, the Geonic period, public discourses were held on *Shabbat* afternoons. Thus, the idea of including into the service some learning, in the form of *Mishnah*, clearly derived from that practice. Since the main discourse preceded *Minchah*, in order not to overtax the minds of the public with another heavy discourse between *Minchah* and *Ma-ariv*, they introduced some light, moral exhortation, in the form of *Pirkei Avot*, at this time.

The *Mishnah Avot* contains only five chapters. When the academy of Sura introduced it into the liturgy, they appended a sixth chapter, taken from a post-Talmudic ethical work. It bears the name *Beraita of Rabbi Meir*, since it commences with a quotation in his name. It is also referred to as *Perek Kinyan Torah*, the chapter regarding the acquisition of *Torah*, since this is its central theme. Its first recitation, coinciding with the *Shabbat* before the festival of *Shavuot*, made this chapter, in praise of the *Torah*, a most appropriate one with which to herald the approach of the festival which commemorates the giving of the *Torah* on Mount Sinai.

Before commencing each chapter, we recite the affirmation כָּל יִשְׂרָאֵל יֵשׁ לָהֶם חֵלֶק לָעוֹלָם הַבָּא, "All Israel have a portion in the World to Come". The reason for this statement, it has been suggested, was to pacify and comfort those who were ignorant of the *Torah*, so that they should not feel that a share in the World to Come is dependent upon intellectual attainment.

At the end of each chapter we recite a statement in the name of רַבִּי חֲנַנְיָא בֶּן עֲקַשְׁיָא. Whereas Christianity asserted that the *Torah*, with its manifold laws, was a burden imposed upon wayward Israel for her lack of true faith, and denial of the Christian Saviour, Rabbi Hananya insisted that, since the performance of every additional commandment brings with it an added reward, it was a conscious act of favour on the part of God that He provided Israel with so many commandments to observe, and so much potential reward to reap.

It is possible that this section was also included to appease those with little Jewish learning. It is the observance of the commandments, says Rabbi Hananya, that "makes Israel worthy", not Rabbinic knowledge.

After the *Chazan* has recited the Rabbi Hananya section, the mourners recite *Kaddish d'Rabbanan*, (page 31 [52]). This is followed by the *Aleinu*, after which the Mourner's *Kaddish* is recited.

page 473-475
[526-528]

XIII

Service for the Conclusion of Shabbat
עַרְבִית לְמוֹצָאֵי שַׁבָּת

page 533 [592]   The congregation sings psalms 144 and 67, in order that the leave-taking of the *Shabbat* should be to the accompaniment of song, in the same manner as it was welcomed. Another function served by the recitation of these psalms is to delay, for a moment, the termination of the holy day, in conformity with the Talmudic principle that it is a *Mitzvah* to add on to the *Shabbat* from the weekday.

The appropriateness of the first psalm is apparent from its opening verse, "Blessed be the Lord, my Rock, who teaches my hands to war and my fingers to fight". We are reminded, most forcefully, that the tranquillity of the *Shabbat* inevitably gives way to the arduous, and on occasions, cruel, competitive fight for material survival during the six working days ahead.

Psalm 67 opens with a paraphrase of the familiar Priestly Benediction, "May God be gracious unto us, and bless us; may He make his face to shine upon us". This serves to invoke the Divine blessing upon our efforts during the week ahead.

page 535-561 [256-278]   The Evening Service is exactly as on weekdays, from וְהוּא רַחוּם. (See above, pages 76 to 79). A mourner is given the privilege of acting as Reader in this service.

The *Havdalah* blessing, אַתָּה חוֹנַנְתָּנוּ, is recited in the middle of the blessing commencing אַתָּה חוֹנֵן. The latter is a petition for knowledge and understanding, and was considered appropriate as the context for *Havdalah*, since, "Without knowledge, *Havdalah* ('distinction', between holy and profane) is impossible" (*Talmud*).

119

Service for the Conclusion of Shabbat

One may question why a *Havdalah* blessing is required at all, since there is a special *Havdalah* ceremony at the end of the Service. It has been suggested that it was introduced during a period of drought and poverty, when wine could not be obtained for the *Havdalah* ceremony. When prosperity returned and the ceremony was reintroduced, the blessing was omitted, only to be reintroduced when drought struck again. Instead of having the blessing *in reserve*, it finally won a permanent place in the Service, in spite of the repetition involved.

page 561 [594] After the congregation has completed the silent *Amidah*, the Reader recites the half-*Kaddish*. The service continues with וִיהִי נֹעַם, followed by וְאַתָּה קָדוֹשׁ. These sections are omitted if a festival occurs on any working day of the following week. This is because the phrase וּמַעֲשֵׂה יָדֵינוּ כּוֹנְנָה עָלֵינוּ ("Establish for us the work of our hands") was understood to refer to the full working week. Where 'the work of our hands' is interrupted for a festival, it was considered inappropriate to recite these sections.

page 565 [598] The Reader recites aloud the concluding verse:

יְיָ חָפֵץ לְמַעַן צִדְקוֹ, יַגְדִּיל תּוֹרָה וְיַאְדִּיר,,

followed by the full-*Kaddish* (page 459 [598]).

From the evening before the second day of *Pesach*, until *Shavuot*, we count the *Omer* each night. On *Shabbat* nights it is counted here, and on *Chanukah* the candles are lit in synagogue at this stage in the Service.

page 567 [600] The section commencing וְיִתֶּן לְךָ is recited silently by the congregation. It is comprised exclusively of Biblical verses which assure Israel of Divine blessing. In Israel and several Diaspora communities it is no longer said.

page 573 [606] The section commencing: אָמַר רַבִּי יוֹחָנָן adduces verses from the three divisions of the Bible to prove that wherever God's greatness and majesty is described, a

120

page 573 [608]

reference to His loving care for the less fortunate of His creatures is also included. It has been suggested that this section is added to remind us, as we embark upon a new week of business activity, that God cares for the lowly and the poor, and that He will not tolerate any financial exploitation of them. The section ends with psalm 128 which emphasizes the satisfaction that can be obtained through hard work: "When you eat the labour of your hands, happy shall you be". It continues that only by serious effort shall a man establish himself and crown his happiness with a wife and children. The psalmist ends by invoking the blessing of longevity and peace.

The Havdalah Ceremony

page 579 [618]

The *Chazan* then recites the *Havdalah* ceremony. This should also be performed by the male head of the household when he returns home from synagogue, for the benefit of his family. When *Havdalah* is recited at home, we commence with הִנֵּה אֵל יְשׁוּעָתִי. In the synagogue, however, the *Chazan* commences with the blessing over wine. Some have the custom to use beer for the purpose of *Havdalah*, though wine is certainly preferable. As a symbol of prosperity the cup is filled to overflowing, and held, as always, in the right hand.

Before commencing *Havdalah*, we light a candle, which is usually given to a child to hold. We also take a box containing spices, the fragrances of which are inhaled during the ceremony.

The word *Yabneh* is mentioned as an aid to remember the sequence of the blessings, which is Yayin (wine); Besamim (spices); Ner (light); Havdalah (the final blessing of distinction).

A mystical reason for the spices is that they serve to revive the spirit, which is depressed by the imminent departure of the *Shabbat*. The Holy Day is supposed to suffuse Israel with a *Neshamah Yeteirah*, an additional,

121

up-lifting spirit. With the departure of *Shabbat* we are bereft of this, and feel slightly depressed at having to return to the mundane sphere of activity. The fragrant spices help to soothe our anxious spirit as we contemplate the problems of the week ahead.

A more practical explanation is that *Havdalah* represents the conclusion of the last *Shabbat* meal, in the same way as the Friday night *Kiddush* marked the commencement of the first meal. In Talmudic times they used to conclude a meal by placing aromatic spices upon burning coals, to dispel the smells of cooking and food in the living/dining room. Since this could not be done on the *Shabbat*, they waited until the *Shabbat* had terminated. Thus, the burning of spices came, in time, to be associated with the termination of the *Shabbat*, and ultimately won a place in the *Havdalah* ceremony.

Light was produced on the first day of Creation; hence we kindle a light to usher in the first day of the week. The candle also serves to denote that the *Shabbat*, during which it was forbidden to kindle any fire, has now terminated. It is customary to raise one's fingernails towards the light in order to catch the reflection. In this way we justify the reciting of the benediction by actually making use of the light.

The blessing over the light, בּוֹרֵא מְאוֹרֵי הָאֵשׁ, literally means 'who created the *lights* of the fire'. On the basis of this the Rabbis have declared a single flame to be insufficient. In order to give a torch-like appearance, it is customary to use a plaited candle for *Havdalah*.

page 575 [608]   The service concludes, after *Havdalah*, with *Aleinu*, followed by the Mourner's *Kaddish*.

At the conclusion of the Service one greets one's neighbour with the traditional greeting '*Shavua Tov*' ('a good week'). The Yiddish form of greeting, '*Gut Voch*', is still widely used.

122

XIV

You're Late. Where Are They Up To? How Do You Catch Up?

In this chapter we shall try to offer guidance as to the particular place in the service that the congregation will be at, and what to omit in order to catch up if one comes late to synagogue. Obviously this cannot be precise, since it depends upon how slowly or rapidly the one leading the service proceeds.

THE WEEKDAY SERVICE

How Much Late	The congregation will be at:	Page
5 minutes	Mourner's *Kaddish* at the end of *Korbanot* (sacrificial section).	31 [52]
8 minutes	*Ashrei* (psalm 145).	43 [66]
12 minutes	Towards the end of the *Shirah* (Song of the Red Sea).	57 [80]
20 minutes	The recitation of the silent *Amidah*.	75-89 [98-118]
24 minutes	The beginning of the Reader's repetition of the *Amidah*.	75 [98]
28 minutes	The end of the Reader's repetition of the *Amidah*.	83-89 [110-116]

(On fast days, if it is the custom of your synagogue to recite the special *S'lichot* in the middle of the *S'lach lanu* blessing of the repetition of the *Amidah*, then the remaining times, in column one, will have to be adjusted accordingly. Clearly, someone arriving 25 minutes late for the service on a fast day will find the congregation having just commenced the *S'lichot*, rather than, as on other days, nearing the end of the service.)

123

You're Late. Where Are They Up To?
How Do You Catch Up?

How Much Late	The congregation will be at:	Page
30 minutes	On Mondays and Thursdays: at the end of the extended *Tachanun*. On those days when *Hallel* is recited: in the middle of that section.	107-109 [136-138] 585-593 [532-642]
	On other weekdays, commencing *Ashrei*.	23 [150]
35 minutes	On Mondays and Thursdays: concluding the reading of the *Torah*.	
	On other weekdays: approaching the end of the service.	133-143 [158-168]
	On those days when *Hallel* is recited, since *Tachanun* is omitted, the service will also be at the point of the Reading of the *Torah*.	
40 minutes	On ordinary Mondays, Thursdays and festive days without *Musaf*: approaching the end of the service.	
	On those days when *Musaf* is recited: commencing the *Musaf Amidah* of either *Rosh Chodesh* or *Chol ha-Mo-ed*.	595 [644] 639 [674]
45 minutes	Commencing the Reader's repetition of the respective *Musaf Amidah*.	
50 minutes	Commencing *Ashrei*.	123 [150]
55 minutes	Concluding the service.	133 [158]

124

You're Late. Where Are They Up To?

How Do You Catch Up?

THE *SHABBAT* AND FESTIVAL SERVICES

How Much Late	The congregation will be at:	Page
5 minutes	The end of the *Korbanot* (sacrificial section).	27-31 [47-52]
10 minutes	*Lamnatze-ach mizmor.*	295 [374]
15 minutes	*Hodu.*	303[384]
20 minutes	*Halleluyah hallelu et Adonai.*	315 [394]
25 minutes	*Nishmat.*	323 [400]
30 minutes	*El adon.*	331 [410]
35 minutes	The middle of the *Shema.*	337-343 [414-420]
40 minutes	The end of the silent *Amidah.*	357 [430]
45 minutes	The middle of the Reader's repetition of the *Amidah.*	345-357 [420-430]
50 minutes	*Ein Kamocha* and the taking out of the *Sefer Torah.*	361-365 [432-436]
	On festive days, when *Hallel* is recited: in the middle of that section.	585-591 [632-642]

Note: A cantorial and/or choral *Hallel* can well throw our timing for the rest of the service well out of sync! We are allowing 20 minutes here for its recitation.

You're Late. Where Are They Up To?
How Do You Catch Up?

How Much Late	The congregation will be at:	Page
70 minutes	On festive days (when *Hallel* is added): at *Ein Kamocha* and the taking out of the *Sefer Torah*.	361-365 [432-436]
	On an ordinary *Shabbat*: around *sh'lishi* (third of the seven call-ups to the *Torah*).	
2 hours	The recitation of the *Haftarah*.	
2 hrs 15 mins	Prayer for the Royal Family. Prayer for the State of Israel.	381 381-382

Note: A cantorial and/or choral Blessing for the New Moon (383 [452]) may add an extra seven minutes to our calculations for the remainder of the service.

2 hrs 25 mins	The return of the *Sefer Torah*. to the *Aron Kodesh*.	

Note: On festivals, the shorter reading from the *Torah* compensates for the recitation of *Hallel*, making the timing approximately the same at this point, both on *Shabbat* and festivals.

The sermon is, obviously, a variable. We allow 10 minutes (You should be so lucky!!) here in our calculations.

2 hrs 35 mins	The commencement of the silent *Musaf Amidah*, for a regular *Shabbat* or for festivals.	395 [462] 639 [674]
2 hrs 40 mins	Reader's repetition of the *Musaf Amidah*.	413 [476]
3 hrs	*Adon Olam*.	425 [12]

You're Late. Where Are They Up To?

How Do You Catch Up?

HOW DO YOU CATCH UP?

At the outset, may I make it clear that this chapter should not be construed as condoning late arrival to synagogue. Nothing can justify that. People who would not dream of being late for school, for a lecture, a business meeting or for the theatre, for some reason have no qualms about appearing late in synagogue for an audience with the King of Kings! The advice below is given, simply, because, as long as the majority of people are, indeed, remiss in this matter, there is no point in ignoring the situation and allowing them to compound their offence by doing the wrong thing when they finally get to synagogue. So, please regard this information as 'To be used only in an emergency'!

As we have already observed, whenever the *Talmud* speaks of 'Prayer', it refers, almost exclusively, to the *Amidah*. That prayer, with its nineteen blessings, expresses all the personal and national petitions that are of concern to the Jew, as well as the most appropriate form of praise and thanksgiving to God. So important is this prayer, that a repetition was introduced for the benefit of those who could not recite it by heart (in an age when there were no printed prayer books), to ensure that they were able to hear it word for word from the Reader, and to fulfil their duty by mentally affirming his words of Prayer. It is therefore a supreme consideration that, to maximize on the collective effectiveness of these petitions, every worshipper present in synagogue should be reciting the *Amidah* at the same time.

For late-comers it is especially important, therefore, that they know how to 'catch up', in order to achieve this. Clearly it will be necessary to skip less essential parts of the service. But how much is omitted is dependent upon how far ahead the congregation is when one arrives at synagogue. However, since it is not proper to recite the *Shema* after the *Amidah*, the objective has to be shifted, namely, to attempt to recite the *Shema* (and its blessings) also together with the congregation. Thus, once *Bor'chu* has been recited, he should be joining the congregation and not attempting to make up what he has missed. (Because the *Shema* has to precede the *Amidah*, anyone arriving in synagogue to find the congregation commencing the *Amidah* may not join in with them and recite the *Shema* later, but must first recite the *Shema* and its blessings.)

There is one proviso, however, when it comes to joining in with the congregation at a later stage, or, with a little more time to spare, making a

127

You're Late. Where Are They Up To?

How Do You Catch Up?

selection of prayers; and that is that, under all circumstances, the late-comer must immediately recite the early blessings of *Al netilat yadayim,* *Asher yatzar,* the three *Torah* blessings (*La-asok b'divrei Torah; V'ha-arev na* and *Asher bachar banu* (13 [14-15]) and the *Elohai n'shamah* (15 [18]).

If he has time, he should then proceed to *Baruch She-amar* (289 [370]), which constitutes the introductory blessing to the whole of the next section of the service: the *P'sukei d'Zimra* (passages from the psalms), and he should then recite at least one of those psalms. *Ashrei* (309 [390]) is the most important psalm, and that is the one that should be recited in this situation. He should then continue with *Yishtabach* (327 [404]) - being the closing blessing over the psalms - and join the congregation in the recitation of *Bor'chu* (329 [406]) and the rest of the service.

If he has some more time available, to recite some extra psalms before the congregation reaches *Bor'chu,* priority should be given to the *Halleluyah* psalms (311-317 [392-396]). If he still has time to catch up further, he should include the following, in descending order of importance: *Vay'varech David* until *l'sheim tif'artecha* (317 [396]); *Hodu l'Adonai kir'u vishmo* until *V'hu rachum* (291-293 [370-372] [paragraph 3]); and, if time still permits, the *Shirat ha-Yam* from *Vayosha* (319-323 [398-400]).

On *Shabbat,* late-comers should give priority to *Nishmat* (323 [400]) and to the psalms recited on weekday mornings, since their greater frequency of recitation invests them with extra importance. If he has time to recite some extra prayers, and still catch up with the congregation at *Bor'chu,* he should recite *Lamnatze-ach, L'David b'shanoto* and *T'fillah l'Mosheh* (295-299 [374-380]). The psalms that one has had to omit may be recited at the conclusion of the service.

If he is left with no time to recite any of the earlier psalm section, such as when the Reader and congregation have already recited *Bor'chu,* he should join in at that point. If, however, he arrives as the congregation is approaching the silent *Amidah,* he may *not* join with them and recite the *Shema* (and blessings) later, since we have an important principle, *S'michat G'ulah lit'fillah,* that the *Shema* and its concluding blessing (*Ga-al Yisrael*) must *precede* the *Amidah.* This principle is not as strictly applied to *Ma-ariv* however, when the silent *Amidah* may be recited (by a late-comer) prior to the *Shema* and its blessings.

128

XV

Selections from the Laws
of Mourning

The period of formal mourning for parents extends over a full year. The period of mourning for a wife, husband, son, daughter, brother or sister extends for only thirty days, called *Sh'loshim*.

Shivah, seven days of house-bound mourning, commences immediately after the burial. The day of burial is reckoned as one complete day of the *Shivah* period. Similarly, on the seventh day, the mourner need sit for only one hour, being the duration of the Morning Service, after which the *Shivah* is regarded as complete, and normal work may be resumed.

Before the burial, *K'riah*, the rending of one's garment, is performed. For parents, the tear is made on the left side (near the heart); for other near relatives, on the right side. The *K'riah* garment is not worn on *Shabbat*, since all outward expressions of mourning are forbidden on that day.

If one receives news of the death of any of the near relatives (listed above) within thirty days, *Shivah* and *Sh'loshim* (the succeeding 23 days of lesser mourning) are observed in the normal way. If, however, news of death is delayed until a full 30 days have elapsed, then *Shivah* is not observed. In such a case the mourner merely removes his shoes, sits on a low stool for one hour and, in the case of the demise of a parent, rends his garment.

All mirrors in a house of mourning are covered up. A mourner is not permitted to wear leather shoes, shave or have a haircut, cohabit, or wear new, or freshly laundered, garments. He should not take a hot bath, but may shower. A *Yahrzeit* light is kept burning throughout the week of *Shivah*, and two candles are lit before each service commences.

Any festival occurring during the *Shivah* period has the effect of annulling the rest of the *Shivah*, provided that the mourners were able to commence their *Shivah*, even for a brief period, before the onset of the festival. If death occurs during a festival (or on *Chol ha-Mo-ed*, the intermediate days), *Shivah* is not commenced until the termination of the festival. In such circumstances, the last day of the festival is deducted from the *Shivah* period, thus reducing it to a six-day observance.

When mourning a parent, it is forbidden to attend a place of celebration or entertainment or listen to music for twelve months. In the case of other near relatives the prohibition is for thirty days. *Kaddish* is recited for 11 months. The *Yahrzeit* is observed on the anniversary of the Jewish date of death. Although it is customary in Britain to erect a tombstone only after the 11 months have elapsed, there is no law to this effect. It may, in fact, be erected at any time during the year.

The above selection is merely for general information. The guidance of a Rabbi should always be sought when questions of Jewish law arise.

XVI

How to Observe a *Yahrzeit*

Yahrzeit is a day of sacred commemoration, marked by the lighting of a special memorial light and attendance at synagogue for the recitation of the Mourner's *Kaddish*. *Kaddish* is recited at the Evening Service on the eve of the *Yahrzeit*. Since the *Yahrzeit* does not occur on the same civil date each year, it is the responsibility of the synagogue office to send an annual reminder to members of the dates of their *Yahrzeits*.

One should not listen to music or attend a place of entertainment on one's *Yahrzeit*. It should be observed as a solemn day of nostalgic recollection, of *Torah* study and the giving of charity. It is also regarded as a most appropriate time for visiting the grave of the departed.

It is obligatory to call a person up to the Reading of the *Torah* on the day of his *Yahrzeit*. It is also customary to call him up on the *Shabbat* morning preceding the *Yahrzeit*, when a special memorial prayer (*Eil malei rachamim*) is recited. Where the one observing the *Yahrzeit* has the ability, he has priority for acting as Reader to lead the services. If possible, he should also lead the preceding Saturday night *Ma-ariv* service.

The memorial candle is lit at nightfall on the evening of the *Yahrzeit*, and is left to burn itself out, rather than being extinguished at the conclusion of the *Yahrzeit*. Below we offer some meditations, in English, which may be recited after lighting the *Yahrzeit* candle.

Yahrzeit in the month of Adar

Where one's relative has passed away in *Adar* of an ordinary (ie non-leap) year, the *Yahrzeit* is observed on the same Hebrew date in an ordinary year. In a leap year, however, when there are two months of *Adar*, it is the general custom to observe the *Yahrzeit* on the corresponding day of the *first Adar*. (Some have the practice of also reciting *Kaddish* on the corresponding day of the second *Adar*.)

Where one's relative has passed away in either *Adar* I or *Adar* II of a leap year, then, in an ordinary year *Yahrzeit* is observed on the corresponding day of *Adar*. In a leap year, however, it is observed in the particular *Adar* in which death occurred. Thus, if the person died on the tenth day of *Adar* I, then that will be the date of the *Yahrzeit* in a leap year. If death occurred on the tenth day of *Adar* II, then that will be the date of the *Yahrzeit*.

MEDITATIONS

FOR A HUSBAND OR WIFE

> *Father of mercy, look down upon me as I stand this day, paying fond and reverent tribute to the memory of my beloved husband/wife ... (insert here the name of the departed).*
>
> *Oh, how I miss my twin soul and partner, who shared with me all my dreams and confidences, and who walked lovingly and proudly at all times by my side, making the joys we shared so much sweeter, and the sorrows so much easier to bear. Oh, how I miss the companionship, the love, kindness, generosity and support which he/she gave, and which I gratefully recall at this sacred moment.*
>
> *Almighty God, only You really know how much light has been removed from my life since his/her passing. Send me, therefore, Your soothing comfort, and compensate me with Your protection, Your love and Your blessing, until the moment of reunion arrives.*
>
> *Send me the gift of health and strength so that I will not become a burden to others, especially to those I love. Give me good reason, Lord, to be joyful and to bless Your name.*
>
> *Amen.*

FOR A CHILD

Father of mercy, look down upon me as I stand this day, paying loving tribute to the memory of my beloved child ... who was taken from me so tragically before his/her life had run its normal course.

I do not presume to understand the mystery of life and death, nor to call into question the righteousness of Your will. Man's pilgrimage on earth is, after all, to serve Your sovereign and unfathomable purpose. Indeed, from that do I draw strength and courage, in the knowledge that the period of my beloved child's existence on earth was pre-determined by You according to a sacred plan. All that You do is for the best, and in my grief I humbly acknowledge Your righteousness.

Help me, Lord, to bear my burden without complaint, without giving in to despair, without spreading gloom. Renew within me the will to smile, and to look forward to the future with hope, joy and confidence.

My child's soul is committed to Your loving care. It lives on with You, enjoying the rewards that are treasured up for the innocent and the righteous. That I do believe, and for that I shall hope until the day of reunion arrives.

God bless his/her immortal soul forever.

Amen.

FOR PARENTS

Father of mercy, look down upon me as I stand this day, paying fond and reverent tribute to the memory of my beloved father/mother/parents...

Each soul that you have created is unique and unbounded in its capacity to give love and to radiate joy. When that soul is removed from among us, the quality of our lives is sorely diminished.

The nature of man is to take for granted the love that is shown to him, and the sacrifices made for him, by his parents. Frequently it is only in retrospect that the magnitude of their gifts to us is appreciated. And then it is too late to say "thank you".

But if the soul You have created is immortal, and if death cannot wound it nor the grave suppress its vitality, then my thanks and appreciation are yet heard and my prayers are not in vain. If the soul yet lives with Almighty God, then my debt can still be re-paid by my leading an exemplary life, by studying Your sacred Torah and by rearing my children to be loyal to Your sacred name.

May my beloved father/mother/parents rest in peace, content in the knowledge that his/her/their memory is still revered and beloved in my heart and vivid in my mind and in that of all the family.

Amen.

FOR A SISTER OR BROTHER

> *Father of mercy, look down upon me as I stand this day, paying a fond and reverent tribute to the memory of my beloved sister/brother...*

> *I recall with gratitude the years of our childhood, and the bond which linked us as we shared confidences and hopes, as we helped each other to develop and mature and as we inherited together the valued traditions of our parental home.*

> *And even in later years, when we were separately preoccupied with the task of establishing a career and building our own family life, that bond of love and esteem remained strong.*

> *May my beloved sister/brother rest in peace, content in the knowledge that her/his memory is still revered and beloved in my heart, and vivid in my mind forever.*

> *Amen.*

Conclude with appropriate Memorial prayer, from the standard *Yizkor* service (pages 825 to 828 [810 to 814]).

A NOTE ON TRANSLITERATION

To readers who will be availing themselves of the transliterated prayers in the chapter entitled 'Hebrew Prayers for Non-Hebrew Readers', I offer, at the very outset, this disclaimer. Transliteration is not a precise art. It is simply not possible to convey in English the exact vowel sounds that are used in Hebrew, and, in particular, the subtle distinctions between some similar-sounding vowels.

Furthermore, we have the overriding problem of deciding which particular Hebrew pronunciation we wish to convey. The Central-European Ashkenazi? The Polish Ashkenazi? Russian Ashkenazi? The Spanish and Portuguese Sephardi, as read by the Sephardim of England? If the answer to this query is: obviously the Hebrew of the State of Israel, then my reader is reminded of the fact that the entire spectrum of pronunciation may be heard in that melting-pot of contemporary Jewry.

We have not attempted to choose any one particular mode, and certainly not to convey any tincture of the guttural Hebrew, brought to Israel by our Oriental Sephardi brethren. Our narrow, though primary, objective has been, simply, to enable our readers to employ Hebrew as a medium of Prayer. Within the multiplicity of modes of Hebrew pronunciation, we simply cannot apply the criteria of 'correct' or 'incorrect'.

Fully aware of its limitations, we have sought to distinguish between the two vowels *cholam,* as in the word הוֹדוֹ, (*hohdoh*) and *kamatz,* as in the word דָבָר, (*davar*), notwithstanding the fact that in rapid, spoken Hebrew, this distinction is quite subtle. Thus we have employed '*oh*' to denote the *cholam* and '*a*' to denote the *kamatz* sound.

Where, in transliteration, two vowels come together, we have employed the hyphen to avoid them being elided, as in normal English. We have also employed the apostrophe sign to denote the sounded *sheva,* as in בְּרָכָה, (*b'rachah*) which approximates the 'e' in the French word '*le*'.

Those relying exclusively on this book for guidance as to the correct pronunciation of Hebrew are advised to seek help from a fluent Hebrew reader to ensure that they are on right lines. *Hatzlachah Rabbah!* Good Luck!

XVII

Key to the Hebrew Alphabet

(Modern, Sephardic Pronunciation)

Letter	Name	Sound
א	Alef	none
בּ	Bet	b - as in 'book'
ב	Vet	v - as in 'very'
ג	Gimmel	g - as in 'goat'
ד	Dalet	d - as in 'day'
ה	Hey	h - as in 'hole'
ו	Vav	v - as in 'very'
ז	Zayin	z - as in 'zoo'
ח	Chet	ch - as in (Scottish) 'loch'
ט	Tet	t - as in 'table'
י	Yod	y - as in 'year'
כּ	Kaf	k - as in 'king'
כ	Chaf	ch - as in (Scottish) 'loch'
ך	Final Chaf	ch - as in (Scottish) 'loch'
ל	Lammed	l - as in 'land'
מ	Mem	m - as in 'man'
ם	Final Mem	m - as in 'man'
נ	Nun	n - as in 'name'
ן	Final Nun	n - as in 'name'
ס	Samech	s - as in 'sun'
ע	Ayin	None

פ	Pey	p - as in 'pan'
פ	Fey	f - as in 'fun'
ף	Final Fey	f - as in 'fun'
צ	Tsadi	ts - as in 'bats'
ץ	Final Tsadi	ts - as in 'bats'
ק	Kuf	k - as in 'king'
ר	Reysh	r - as in 'ran'
שׁ	Shin	sh - as in 'show'
שׂ	Sin	s - as in 'sun'
ת	Taf	t - as in 'table'

VOWELS

Vowel	Sound
◻	a - as in 'at'
◻	a - as in 'at' (but occasionally o - as in 'hot')
◻	eh - as in 'bed'
◻	ay - as in 'say'
◻	i - as in 'lid'
◻	u - as in 'bull'
◻	e - as in (French) 'le'
וּ	u - as in 'bush'
וֹ	o - as in 'oh'

XVIII

Test Your Hebrew
Reading Skills

Here are some Hebrew words and their pronunciation. Use them to practise your Hebrew reading. Cover up the right-hand transliterated column, read each word of the left-hand column and then test yourself to see if you had the correct pronunciation.

Remember: The transliterated 'ch' is to be pronounced
as in the Scottish 'loch'

The ' sign in this list is to be pronounced
as in the French definite article 'le'.

אַב	*av*	הִיא	*hiy*
בָּא	*ba*	זָבָה	*zavah*
אַבָּא	*aba*	אַוְוז	*avaz*
בִּי	*biy*	הוֹד	*hohd*
בָּבָא	*bava*	טוֹב	*tohv*
בָּה	*bah*	הַטֶּה	*hateih*
בָּז	*baz*	הַבֵּט	*habeit*
גַד	*gad*	יְהִי	*y'hiy*
דוֹב	*dohv*	יִיטַב	*yiytav*
דָג	*dag*	כָּבוֹד	*kavohd*
זוּג	*zug*	חֵטְא	*cheit*

Test Your Hebrew Reading Skills

בָּזָה	*bazah*	חַג	*chag*
הוּבָא	*huvah*	חֶדְוָה	*chedvah*
כַּד	*kad*	עֲבָדִים	*avadim*
כֹּחַ	*koh-ach*	פֶּן	*pen*
זַךְ	*zach*	פָּנִים	*panim*
הַךְ	*hach*	בָּנִים	*banim*
כֹּל	*kohl*	מָעוֹן	*m'ohn*
בְּלִי	*b'liy*	בְּכָל	*b'chol*
זְבוּל	*z'vul*	לְבָבְךָ	*l'vav'cha*
חֶבְלֵי	*chevlei*	וְהָיוּ	*v'hayu*
מִמְּךָ	*mimcha*	הָאֵלֶה	*ha-eileh*
חֲלוֹם	*chalohm*	אָנֹכִי	*anohchiy*
מוֹדֶה	*mohdeh*	אַף	*af*
חֵן	*chein*	כַּף	*kaf*
בִּנְךָ	*bincha*	מִצְוָה	*mitzvah*
סוֹד	*sohd*	צוֹפֶה	*tzohfeh*
בְּסוֹד	*b'sohd*	פּוֹצֶה	*pohtzeh*
סֻלָם	*sulam*	קֵץ	*keitz*
סְבִיבוֹן	*s'vivohn*	קוּמִי	*kumiy*
עוֹד	*ohd*	חֲנוּכָּה	*chanukah*
מְאֹד	*m'ohd*	אֲרוֹמִמְךָ	*arohmimcha*

הוֹפִיעַ	hohfiya	מֶלֶךְ	melech
פַּחְדְּךָ	pachd'cha	וְקַיָּם	v'kayyam
בְּחֶמְלָה	b'chemlah	קְדוּשָׁה	k'dushah
חָכְמָה	chochmah	לְקָדוֹשׁ	l'kadohsh
בָּרָא	bara	מַעֲשִׂים	ma-asim
הָאָרֶץ	ha-aretz	בָּרוּךְ	baruch
נַפְשְׁךָ	nafsh'cha	חָפֵץ	chafeitz
אֲשֶׁר	asher	תְּפִילִין	t'fillin
פְּרִי	p'riy	קְטוֹרֶת	k'tohret
שׁוֹשׁ	sohs	וְהַמִּתְנַשֵּׂא	v'hamitnasei
הַגֶּפֶן	hagafen	מִשְׁתַּחֲוִים	mishtachavim
סְגוּלָה	s'gulah	וּמַצְמִיחַ	umatzmi-ach
שׁוֹמֵר	shohmer	מֵישָׁרִים	meisharim
שְׁמַע	sh'ma	וְלִמְקַלְלַי	v'limkal'lai
נִשְׁאַרְנוּ	nisharnu	הַחוֹשְׁבִים	hachoshvim
תָּם	tam	קְדוּשָׁתְךָ	k'dushat'cha
טָהוֹר	tahohr	הַמַּעֲרִיב	hama-ariv
שְׁאֵרִית	sh'eirit	וְנִשְׂמַח	v'nismach
בְּשִׁלוּשׁ	b'shilush	תִּשְׁבָּחוֹת	tishbachoht

XIX

Hebrew Prayers for
Non-Hebrew Readers

We have included this section on account of the fact that there are some people who attend *Shabbat* morning services, but who cannot read Hebrew. Their spiritual uplift could be considerably heightened, and their embarrassment reduced, if they were able to join in with the congregation in the recitation of at least some of the Hebrew prayers, and particularly those sections of the service which are sung aloud by *Chazan* and congregation. The scope of this book has allowed us to provide only a limited selection of these prayers, but we hope they prove helpful.

We trust, however, that those who avail themselves of this section, will not rely on it as a solution to the problem, but that it will motivate them to enrol immediately for a course in Hebrew reading. The technique of teaching people to read is now so developed that fluency is achieved within five or six weeks; and following the synagogue service should inevitably be achieved before very long. Ironically, the objective of this chapter will be realised the sooner it can be dispensed with!

We include a selection of home rituals that are not strictly within the parameter of the synagogue service, with which this book is primarily concerned. We are making the assumption, however, that those interested enough to learn to follow the *Shabbat* services would also wish to inject some religious spirit into their homes by blessing their children, reciting *Kiddush* and saying a selection of the Grace After Meals, particularly those parts to which familiar traditional melodies are sung.

The sign ' is to be pronounced as the 'e' in the French definite article 'le'.
The Hebrew letters ח and כ are rendered here '*ch*' , as in (Scottish) 'loch'.
The sign - is used to indicate a separation between two vowel sounds.
We have used the transliteration '*oh*' to convey the sound
ו or ֹ, as in the English word '*sole*' .
The transliterated form '*ai*' is to be pronounced as in the English 'm*y*' .
The transliterated form '*ei*' is to be pronounced as in the English 's*ay*' .

SELECTION FROM THE MORNING SERVICE

ON AWAKENING:

> *Mohdeh aniy l'fanehcha, melech chai v'kayyam,*
> *Shehechezarta biy nishmatiy b'chemlah.*
> *Rabbah emunatehcha*

> *Tohrah tzivah lanu Mohsheh,*
> *Mohrashah k'hilat ya-akohv.*

ON WASHING THE HANDS:

Recite the following blessing before drying hands:

> *Baruch attah Adohnai Eloh-heinu melech ha-ohlam,*
> *Asher kidshanu b'mitzvohtav, v'tzivanu, al n'tilat yadayim.*

MORNING BLESSINGS:

> *Baruch attah Adohnai, Eloh-heinu, melech ha-ohlam,*
> *asher natan lasechviy viynah, l'havchin bein yohm uvein lailah*
> *Baruch attah Adohnai, Eloh-heinu, melech ha-ohlam, sheloh asaniy nochriy.*
> *Baruch attah Adohnai, Eloh-heinu, melech ha-ohlam,*
> *sheloh asaniy ahved.*

(Men):- *Baruch attah Adohnai, Eloh-heinu, melech ha-ohlam,*
sheloh asaniy ishah.

(Women):- *Baruch attah Adohnai, Eloh-heinu, melech ha-ohlam,*
sheh-asaniy kirtzohnoh.

Baruch attah Adohnai, Eloh-heinu, melech ha-ohlam, pohkei-ach ivriym.
Baruch attah Adohnai, Eloh-heinu, melech ha-ohlam, malbiysh arumim.

144

Baruch attah Adohnai, Eloh-heinu, melech ha-ohlam, matiyr asurim.
Baruch attah Adohnai, Eloh-heinu, melech ha-ohlam, zohkeif k'fufim.
Baruch attah Adohnai, Eloh-heinu, melech ha-ohlam,
rohkah ha-aretz al hamayim.
Baruch attah Adohnai, Eloh-heinu, melech ha-ohlam,
she-asah liy kol tzorkiy.
Baruch attah Adohnai, Eloh-heinu, melech ha-ohlam,
asher heichin mitzadei gaver.
Baruch attah Adohnai, Eloh-heinu, melech ha-ohlam,
ohzeir Yisra-eil bigvurah.
Baruch attah Adohnai, Eloh-heinu, melech ha-ohlam,
ohteir Yisra-eil b'tif'arah.
Baruch attah Adohnai, Eloh-heinu, melech ha-ohlam,
hanohtein laya-eif koh-ach.
Baruch attah Adohnai, Eloh-heinu, melech ha-ohlam,
hama-avir sheinah mei-einai ut'numah mei-af'apai.

KADDISH D'RABBANAN AND MOURNER'S *KADDISH*

(Note: The extra paragraph constituting *Kaddish d'Rabbanan* appears
in the inserted block, below.)

Yitgadal v'yitkadash, sh'mei rabba.
B'alma divra chirutei, v'yamlich malchutei.
B'chayeichohn, uv'yohmeichohn, uv'chayyei dichol
beit Yisra-eil, ba-agala, uvizman kariv,
v'imru, Amen.

Pause here for the congregation to respond with the following line,
then continue:-

Y'hei sh'mei rabba m'varach,
l'alam ul'ohlmei almaya.

Yitbarach, v'yishtabach, v'yitpa-ar, v'yitrohmam,
v'yitnasei, v'yit-hadar, v'yit-aleh, v'yit-hallal, sh'mei dikudsha,
brich hu.

The congregation joins in with last two words.

L'eila min kol birchata v'shirata,
tushb'chata v'nechemata, diy amiran b'alma,
v'imru, Amen.

For *Kaddish d'Rabbanan* only, add:

Al Yisra-eil, v'al rabbanan, v'al talmideihohn,
v'al kol talmidei talmideihohn, v'al kol man diy oskin b'ohraita,
diy b'atra hadein, v'diy b'chol atar v'atar. Y'hei l'hohn ul'chohn,
sh'lama rabba, chinah v'chisdah, v'rachamin,
v'chayin arichin, um'zohna r'vicha,
uforkana, min kadam avuhohn diy vishmaya,
v'imru, Amen.

For both types of *Kaddish*, continue:

Y'hei shlama rabba min sh'maya, v'chayim

(For *Kaddish d'Rabbanan,*
insert here the word: *tohvim*)

aleinu, v'al kol Yisra-eil, v'imru Amen.

When reciting the last line (עֹשֶׂה שָׁלוֹם בִּמְרוֹמָיו), take three steps backwards, then three steps forwards.

Ohseh shalohm bimrohmav, hu

(For *Kaddish d'Rabbanan,*
insert here the word:

b'rachamav)

ya-aseh shalohm, aleinu, v'al kol Yisra-eil,
v'imru Amen.

ASHREI - PSALM 145

(Note: the initial letters of the lines form the *Alef-Bet*, except for *Nun*.)

Ashrei yohshvei veitecha; ohd y'hal'lucha selah.
Ashrei ha-am shekacha loh; ashrei ha-am she-Adohnai Elohav.

T'hilah l'david.

Arohmimcha Eloh-hai hamelech; va-avaracha shimcha l'ohlam va-ed.
B'chol yohm avaracheka; va-ahal'lah shimcha l'ohlam va-ed.
Gadohl Adohnai um'hulal m'ohd; v'ligdulatoh ein cheiker.
Dohr l'dohr y'shabach ma-asecha; ug'vurohtecha yagiydu.
Hadar k'vohd hohdecha; v'divrei nifl'ohtechah asiychah.
Ve-ezuz nohrohtecha yohmeiru; ug'dulat'cha asaprenah.
Zeicher rav tuv'cha yabiyu; v'tzidkat'cha y'raneinu.
Chanun v'rachum Adohnai; erech apayim ug'dal chased.
Tohv Adohnai lakohl; v'rachamav al kol ma-asav.
Yohducha Adohnai kol ma-asecha; vachasidecha y'varachucha.
K'vohd malchut'cha yohmeiru; ug'vurat'cha y'dabeiru.
L'hohdiya livnei ha-adam g'vurohtav; uch'vohd hadar malchutoh.
Malchut'cha malchut kol ohlamim; umemshalt'cha b'chol dohr vadohr.
Sohmeich Adohnai l'chol hanohflim; v'zohkeif l'chol hak'fufim.
Einei chohl eilecha y'sabeiru; v'atta nohtein lahem et ochlam b'itoh.
Pohtei-ach et yadecha; umasbiya l'chol chai ratzohn.
Tzadik Adohnai b'chol d'rachav; v'chasid b'chol ma-asav.
Karohv Adohnai l'chol kohrav; l'chohl asher yikra-uhu ve-emet.
R'tzohn y'rei-av ya-aseh; v'et shavatam yishma v'yohshiyeim.
Shohmeir Adohnai et kol oh-havav; v'eit kol har'sha-im yashmid.
T'hilat Adohnai y'daber piy; viyvareich kol basar sheim kodshoh
l'ohlam va-ed.

Va-anachnu n'vareich Yah; mei-ata v'ad ohlam hal'luyah.

THE *SHEMA*

(Men hold together in their hands the four *Tzitzit* of the *Tallit*.)

First paragraph:

> Sh'ma Yisra-eil, Adohnai Eloh-heinu, Adohnai echad.
> Baruch sheim k'vohd malchutoh l'ohlam va-ed.
>
> V'ahavta eit Adohnai Eloh-hehcha, b'chol l'vav'cha,
> uv'chol nafsh'cha, uv'chol m'ohdehcha.
> V'hayu had'varim ha-eileh, asher anohchiy m'tzav'cha hayohm,
> al l'vavehcha.
> V'shinantam l'vanehcha, v'dibarta bam,
> b'shivt'cha b'veitehcha, uv'lecht'cha vaderech,
> uv'shoch'becha uv'kumehcha.
> Uk'shartam l'oht al yadehcha,
> v'hayu l'tohtafoht bein einecha.
> Uch'tavtam al m'zuzoht beitehcha, uvish'arehcha.

Second paragraph:

> V'hayah iym shamoh-a tishm'u el mitzvohtai
> asher anohchiy m'tzaveh etchem hayohm;
> l'ahavah et Adohnai Eloh-heichem
> ul'ovdoh b'chol l'vav'chem uv'chol nafsh'chem.
> V'natatiy m'tar artz'chem b'itoh, yohreh umalkohsh.
> V'asafta d'ganehcha v'tiyrohsh'cha v'yitzharecha.
> V'natatiy eisev b'sad'cha livhemtecha;
> v'achalta v'savata...
>
> L'ma-an yirbu y'meichem viymei v'neichem al ha-adamah
> asher nishba Adoh-nai la-avohteichem lateit lahem;
> kiymei hashamayim al ha-aretz.

Third paragraph:

Vayohmer Adohnai el mohsheh leimohr.
Dabeir el b'nei yisra'eil v'amarta aleihem,
v'asu lahem tzitzit

(Kiss the *tzitzit*)

al kanfei vigdeihem l'dohrohtam.
V'natnu al tzitzit

(Kiss the *tzitzit*)

hakanaf p'til t'cheilet.
V'hayah lachem l'tzitzit.

(Kiss the *tzitzit*)

Ur'iytem ohtoh;
uz'chartem et kol mitzvoht Adohnai,
va-asiytem ohtam.
V'loh taturu acharei l'vav'chem
v'acharei eineichem
asher attem zohnim achareihem.
L'ma-an tizk'ru va-asiytem et kol mitzvohtai,
vih'yiytem k'dohshim lEiloh-heichem.
Aniy Adohnai Eloh-heichem
asher hohtzeitiy etchem
mei-eretz mitzrayim
lih'yoht lachem lEiloh-him.
Aniy Adohnai Eloh-heichem,
Emet.

THE *AMIDAH*

First blessing:

> *Baruch attah Adohnai, Eloh-heinu, velohei avohteinu,*
> *Eloh-hei avraham, Eloh-hei yitzchak, veiloh-hei ya-akohv;*
> *Ha-Eil hagadohl, haggibohr, v'hanohra, Eil Elyohn,*
> *Gohmeil chasadim tohvim, v'kohnei hakohl,*
> *V'zohcheir chasdei avoht, umeiviy goh-eil liv'nei v'neihem,*
> *L'ma-an sh'moh b'ahavah.*
> *Melech ohzeir umohshi-a umagein.*
> *Baruch attah Adohnai, magein avraham.*

Second blessing:

> *Attah gibohr l'ohlam Adohnai, m'chayei meitim attah rav l'hohshiya.*
> *M'chalkeil chayyim b'chesed, m'chayei meitim b'rachamim rabim;*
> *Sohmeich nohflim v'rohfei chohlim umatiyr asurim,*
> *um'kayeim emunatoh liysheinei afar.*
> *Miy chamohcha ba-al g'vuroht umiy dohmeh lach;*
> *Melech meimit um'chayeh umatzmiyach y'shu-a.*
> *V'ne-eman attah l'hachayoht meitim.*
> *Baruch attah Adohnai, m'chayei hameitim.*

Third Blessing:

> *Attah kadohsh v'shimcha kadohsh uk'dohshim*
> *b'chohl yohm y'hallalucha. Selah.*
> *Baruch attah Adohnai, ha-Eil hakadohsh.*

The *Kedushah*: This responsive 'Sanctification' is recited during the Reader's Repetition of the *Amidah*.

(Congregation, then Reader):

> *N'kadeish et shimcha ba-ohlam, k'sheim shemakdishim ohtoh*
> *bishmei marohm, Kakatuv al yad n'viyecha,*
> *V'kara zeh el zeh v'amar:*

(Congregation):

> *Kadohsh kadohsh kadohsh, Adohnai tz'va-oht,*
> *m'loh chol ha-aretz k'vohdoh*

(Reader):

> *L'umatam baruch yohmeiru*

(Congregation):

> *Baruch k'vohd Adohnai mimkohmoh*

(Reader):

> *Uv'divrei kodsh'cha katuv leimohr*

(Congregation):

> *Yimlohch Adohnai l'ohlam Eloh-hayich tziyohn,*
> *l'dohr vadohr, hal'luyah*

Sixteenth blessing:

> *Sh'ma kohleinu Adohnai Eloh-heinu, chus v'racheim aleinu,*
> *v'kabeil b'rachamim uv'ratzohn et t'filateinu;*
> *Kiy Eil shohmei-a t'filoht v'tachanunim attah,*
> *Umilfanecha malkeinu reikam al t'shiveinu.*
> *Kiy attah shohmei-a t'filat amcha Yisra-eil b'rachamim.*
> *Baruch attah Adohnai, Shohmei-a t'filah.*

Final blessing:

> *Sim shalohm tohvah uv'rachah, chein vachesed,*
> *v'rachamim aleinu, v'al kol Yisra-eil ammehcha.*
> *Bar'cheinu aviynu, kulanu k'echad,*
> *b'ohr panehcha. Kiy v'ohr panehcha natata lanu,*
> *Adohnai Eloh-heinu,*

Tohrat chayyim v'ahavat chesed, utz'dakah, uvr'achah,
v'rachamim v'chayim v'shalohm.
V'tohv b'einecha, l'vareich et ammcha Yisra-eil,
b'chol eit, uv'chol sha-ah, bishlohmehcha.
Baruch attah Adohhnai,
ham'vareich et ammoh Yisra-eil bashalohm.

BLESSINGS ON BEING CALLED UP FOR *TORAH* READING

On Mondays, Thursdays and semi-holy days, the *Torah* is read.
Those called up recite the following blessings:

Before the *Torah* reading:

Bor'chu et Adohnai ham'vohrach
Baruch Adohnai ham'vohrach l'ohlm va-ed.
Baruch attah Adohnai, Eloh-heinu, melech ha-ohlam,
Asher bachar banu mikkol ha-amim,
v'natan lanu et Tohratoh.
Baruch attah Adohnai,
nohtein haTohrah.

After the *Torah* reading:

Baruch attah Adohnai, Eloh-heinu, melech ha-ohlam
asher natan lanu Tohrat emet
v'chayyei ohlam nata b'tohcheinu.
Baruch attah Adohnai,
nohtein haTohrah.

THE *GOHMEIL* BLESSING

Gohmeil is a special thanksgiving blessing for people who have recovered from a serious illness, travelled a long distance by boat or air, or escaped from a situation of danger. It is recited immediately after reciting the concluding blessing over the Torah.

Baruch attah Adohnai, Eloh-heinu melech ha-ohlam
hagohmeil l'chayyavim tohvoht,
sheg'malani kol tohv

The congregation respond with:

Miy sheg'malcha kol tohv,
hu yigmolcha kol tohv, Selah.

ALEINU - THE FIRST PARAGRAPH

Aleinu l'shabei-ach la-adohn hakohl,
lateit g'dulah l'yohtzeir b'reishit.
Sheloh asanu k'gohyei ha-aratzoht,
v'loh samanu k'mishp'choht ha-adamah.
Sheloh sam chelkeinu kahem,
v'gohraleinu k'chol hamohnam.
Va-anachnu kohr'im umishtachavim umohdim,
Lifnei melech malchei ham'lachim,
hakadohsh baruch hu.
Shehu nohteh shamayim v'yohseid aretz,
Umohshav y'karoh bashamayim mima-al,
Ush'chinat uzoh b'gohvhei m'rohmim.
Hu Eloh-heinu, ein ohd;
Emet malkeinu, efes zulatoh.
Kakatuv b'Tohratoh: V'yadata hayohm,
Vahasheivohta el l'vavehcha.
Kiy Adohnai hu ha-eloh-him,
bashamayim mima-al,
v'al ha-aretz mitachat,
Ein ohd.

153

BLESSING ON WASHING THE HANDS BEFORE MEALS

See above, page 144.

GRACE BEFORE MEALS

> *Baruch attah Adohnai Eloh-heinu melech ha-ohlam,*
> *Hamohtziy lechem min ha-aretz.*

GRACE AFTER MEALS

When there are at least three people at table, there is an introductory responsive formula, called *Mezuman,* whereby the one leading the Grace calls upon the others to join him in the prayer.

(Grace leader): *Rabohtai n'vareich.*

(Other diners): *Y'hiy shem Adohnai m'vohrach, mei-attah v'ad ohlam.*

(Grace leader): repeats last response, and continues:

> *Birshut rabbohtai n'vareich*
>
> (where there are at least ten people dining, add here the word *Eloh-heinu*)
>
> *she-achalnu misheloh.*

(Other diners): *Baruch*

> (with ten people dining, add here the word *Eloh-heinu*)
>
> *she-achalnu misheloh uv'tuvoh chayyinu.*

(Grace leader): repeats last response:

(All continue): *Baruch hu uvaruch sh'moh.*

CHORAL SECTIONS OF GRACE

First blessing:

> *Baruch attah Adohnai Eloh-heinu melech ha-ohlam,*
> *Hazan et ha-ohlam kuloh. B'tuvoh, b'chein b'chesed uv'rachamim.*
> *Hu nohtein lechem l'chol basar, kiy l'ohlam chasdoh.*

Uv'tuvoh hagadohl, tamid loh chasar lanu, V'al yechsar lanu,
mazohn l'ohlam va-ed. Ba-avur sh'moh hagadohl,
kiy hu zan um'farneis lakohl, Umeitiv lakohl,
umeichin mazohn, l'chol b'riyohtav asher bara.
Baruch attah Adohnai, hazan et hakohl.

Second blessing:

...Um'farneis ohtanu tamid b'chol yohm, uv'chol eit uv'chol sha-ah.

...Tamid l'ohlam va-ed.
Kakatuv v'achalta v'savata uveirachta et Adohnai Eiloh-hehcha,
Al ha-aretz hatohvah asher natan lach.
Baruch attah Adohnai, al ha-aretz v'al hamazohn.

Third blessing:

...Eloh-heinu avinu, r'einu zuneinu, Farn'seinu v'chalk'leinu,
V'harvicheinu, v'harvach lanu.

... V'na al tatzricheinu, Adohnai Eloh-heinu,
Loh liydei matnat basar vadam,
V'loh liydei halva-atam, Kiy im l'yad'cha, ham'lei-ah, hap'tuchah,
hak'dohshah v'harchavah,
Sheloh neivohsh v'loh nikkaleim, l'ohlam va-ed.

... Uv'nei y'rushalayim iyr hakohdesh bimheirah v'yameinu.
Baruch attah Adohnai, bohneh v'rachamav y'rushalayim,
Amen.

Fourth blessing:

...Ha-Eil avinu malkeinu, adireinu bohreinu
Goh-aleinu yohtzreinu k'dohsheinu k'dohsh ya-akohv,
Roh-einu roh-ei Yisra-eil, hamelech hatohv v'hameitiv lakohl,
Sheb'chol yohm vayohm Hu heitiv, hu meitiv, hu yeitiv lanu.
Hu g'malanu hu gohmleinu hu yigm'leinu la-ad,
L'chein l'chesed ul'rachamim ul'revach, Hatzalah v'hatzlachah,

b'rachah viyshu-a, Nechamah, parnasah v'chalkalah.
V'rachamim v'chayyim v'shalohm v'chol tohv,
Umikkol tohv al y'chasreinu.

...Harachaman, hu yishtabach l'dohr dohrim,
V'yitpa-ar banu l'neitzach n'tzachim,
V'yit-hadar banu la-ad, ul'-ohlmei ohlamim.

...Viyvaser lanu b'sohroht tohvoht y'shu-oht v'nechamoht.

...Kein y'varech ohtanu kulanu yachad, bivrachah sh'leimah,
v'nohmar Amen.

...V'nisa v'rachah mei-eit Adohnai utzdakah mei-Eiloh-hei yisheinu,
V'nimtzah chein v'seichel tohv b'einei Eloh-him v'adam.

On *Shabbat,* festivals and *Rosh Chodesh,* commence: *Migdohl...*

On ordinary days, commence: *Magdil...*

... Y'shu-oht malkoh v'ohseh chesed lim'shichoh
l'david ul'zaroh ad ohlam.
Ohseh shalohm bimrohmav
hu ya-aseh shalohm aleinu v'al kol Yisra-eil,
v'imru Amen.

Final paragraph:

Yiru et Adohnai k'dohshav, kiy ein machsohr liyrei-av.
K'firim rashu v'ra-eivu, v'dohrshei Adohnai loh yachs'ru chol tohv.
Hohdu lAdohnai kiy tohv, kiy l'ohlam chasdoh.
Pohtei-ach et yadehchah, umasbi-a l'chol chai ratzohn.
Baruch hagever asher yivtach bAdohnai, v'hayah Adohnai mivtachoh.
Na-ar hayitiy, gam zakantiy, v'loh ra-iyti tzaddik ne-ezav,
v'zaroh m'vakeish lah-chem. Adohnai ohz l'ammoh yitein,
Adohnai y'varech et ammoh vashalohm.

SELECTION FROM THE WEEKDAY AFTERNOON SERVICE

ASHREI

See above, page 147.

AMIDAH

See above, pages 150 to 151.

Instead of *Sim Shalohm* (page 151), recite the following:

SHALOHM RAV

> Shalohm rav al Yisra-eil am'cha tasim l'ohlam.
> Kiy attah hu melech adohn, l'chol hashalohm.
> V'tohv b'einehcha l'varech et amcha Yisra-eil,
> B'chol eit, uv'chol sha-ah, bishlohmecha. Baruch attah Adohnai,
> ham'varech et ammoh Yisra-eil bashalohm.

ALEINU

See above, page 153.

SELECTION FROM THE WEEKDAY EVENING SERVICE

> V'hu rachum y'chapeir avohn, v'loh yashchit,
> V'hirbah l'hashiv apoh,
> v'loh ya-iyr kol chamatoh.
> Adohnai hohshiya,
> hamelech ya-aneinu v'yohm koreinu.

(In the presence of a *minyan*:

Reader: *Bor'chu et Adohnai ham'vohrach.*)

Congregation: *Baruch Adohnai ham'vohrach l'ohlam va-ed*
Baruch attah Adohnai Eloh-heinu melech ha-ohlam,
asher bidvaroh ma-ariv aravim,
b'chochmah pohteyach sh'-arim,
uvitvunah m'shaneh ittim umachalif et haz'manim,
um'sadeir et hakohchavim b'mishm'roteihem barakiyah kirtzohnoh.
Bohrei yohm valaylah gohleil ohr mipnei chohshech,
v'chohshech mipnei ohr.
Uma-aviyr yohm umeiviy laylah,
umavdiyl bein yohm uvein laylah Adohnai tz'va-oht sh'moh.
Eil chai v'kayyam tamid yimlohch aleinu l'ohlam va-ed.
Baruch attah Adohnai, hama-ariv aravim.

. . . Kiy heim chayeinu v'ohrech yameinu,
uvahem neh'geh yohmam valaylah.
V'ahavat'cha al tasiyr mimmenu l'ohlamim.
Baruch attah Adohnai, oheiv ammoh Yisra-eil.

THE *SHEMA* IS RECITED HERE

(See pages 148 to 149.)

THE *AMIDAH* IS RECITED HERE

(See pages 150 to 151.)

Instead of Sim shalohm (page 151), recite *Shalohm rav* (page 157).

Conclude with *Aleinu* (page 153).

SELECTION FROM THE FRIDAY NIGHT SERVICE

L'CHAH DOHDIY

First verse:

> *Shamohr v'zachohr b'dibur echad, Hishmiyanu Eil ham'yuchad;*
> *Adohnai echad ush'moh echad, L'sheim ul'tiferet v'lit'hilah.*

Refrain:

> *L'chah dohdiy likrat kalah, p'nei Shabbat n'kab'lah.*

Second verse:

> *Likrat Shabbat l'chu v'neilchah, Kiy hiy m'kohr hab'rachah;*
> *Meirohsh mikedem n'suchah, Sohf ma-aseh, b'machashavah t'chilah.*

Refrain - *as above.*

Last verse (recited facing back wall of synagogue):

> *Boh-iy v'shalohm, ateret ba-alah, Gam b'simchah uv'tzahalah;*
> *Tohch emunei am s'gulah, Boh-iy chalah, boh-iy chalah.*

THE PSALM FOR *SHABBAT* (Psalm 92)

> *Mizmohr shir l'yohm hashabbat.*
> *Tohv l'hohdoht lAdohnai ul'zameir l'shimchah elyohn.*
> *L'haggid babohker chasdehchah, v'emunat'chah baleiloht.*
> *Alei asohr, va-alei navel, alei higayohn b'chinohr.*
> *Kiy simachtaniy Adohnai b'fo-olehcha, b'ma-asei yadehcha aranein.*
> *Mah gohdlu ma-asehchah Adohnai, m'ohd omku machsh'vohtehcha.*
> *Ish ba-ar, loh yeidah, uch'sil loh yavin et zoht.*
> *Bifroh-ach r'sha-im k'moh eisev, vayatzitzu kol poh-alei aven,*
> *L'hishohmdam adei ad. V'attah marohm l'ohlam Adohnai.*

Kiy hinnei oyvehcha Adohnai, kiy hinnei oyvehcha yohveidu,
yitpordu kol poh-alei aven.
Vatarem kir'eim karniy, balohtiy b'shemen ra-anan.
Vatabeit einiy b'shurai, bakamim alai m'rei-im, tishma'-na oznai.
Tzadik katamar yifrach, k'erez bal'vanohn yisgeh.
Sh'tulim b'veit Adohnai, b'chatzroht Eloh-heinu yafriychu.
Ohd y'nuvun b'seivah, d'sheinim v'ra-ananim yih'yu.
L'hagid kiy yashar Adohnai, tzuriy, v'loh avlatah boh.

THE *SHEMA*

See above, pages 148 to 149.

V'SHAMRU

V'shamru v'nei Yisra-eil et hashabbat.
La-asoht et hashabbat, l'dohrotam, b'rit ohlam.
Beiniy, uvein b'nei Yisra-eil oht hiy l'ohlam.
Kiy sheishet yamim, asah Adohnai, Et hashamayim v'et ha-aretz,
Uvayohm hash'vi-iy, shavat vayinafash.

SELECTIONS FROM THE *AMIDAH*

First three blessings:

See above, page 150.

Fourth (*Shabbat*) blessing:

Attah kidashta et yohm hash'vi-iy lishmehcha.
Tachlit ma-asei shamayim va-aretz.
Uveirachtoh mikkol hayamim, v'kidashtoh mikkol haz'manim,
V'chein katuv b'Tohratehcha.

(Continue with the *Vay'chulu* section, line 2, to *la-asoht,* line 6, of the *Kiddush,* page 163).

Final blessing:

Shalohm rav, see page 157.

MAGEIN AVOHT

> *Magein avoht bidvaroh,*
> *m'chayei meitim b'ma-amaroh.*
> *Ha-Eil hakadohsh she-ein kamohu,*
> *Hameini-ach l'ammoh b'yohm Shabbat kodshoh.*
> *Kiy vam ratzah l'hani-ach lahem.*
> *L'fanav na-avohd, b'yirah vafachad,*
> *V'nohdeh lishmoh b'chol yohm tamid,*
> *mei-ein habrachoht.*
> *Eil hahohda-oht, adohn hashalohm,*
> *M'kadeish hashabbat um'vareich sh'vi-iy,*
> *Umeini-ach bik'dusha l'am m'dushnei ohneg.*
> *Zeicher l'ma-asei v'reishit.*

ALEINU - THE FIRST PARAGRAPH

See above, page 153.

YIGDAL

(The *Chazan* and congregation sing alternate verses. We reproduce here just the congregation's verses, while indicating only the initial words of the *Chazan*'s lines.)

Yigdal..
Echad, v'ein yachid, k'yichudoh; neh'lam v'gam ein sohf, l'achdutoh.
Ein loh...
Kadmohn l'chol davar, asher nivra; rishohn, v'ein reishit, l'reishitoh.
Hinnoh adohn ohlam...
Shefa n'vu-atoh, n'tanoh; el anshei s'gulatoh umalchutoh.
Loh kam...
Tohrat emet, natan l'ammoh Eil; al yad n'vi-oh, neh-eman beitoh.
Loh yachalif...
Tzohfeh v'yohdei-a, s'tareinu; mabit l'sohf davar, b'kadmatoh.
Gohmeil l'ish...
Yishlach l'keitz yamim, m'shiycheinu; lifdoht m'chakei keitz, y'shu-atoh.
Meitim...
Meitim y'chayeh Eil, b'rohv chasdoh; baruch adei ad, sheim t'hilatoh.

BLESSING OF CHILDREN ON *EREV SHABBAT*, BEFORE *KIDDUSH*

Place both hands on the head of your child and recite the following:

For boys: *Y'simcha Eloh-him k'efrayim v'chimnasheh.*
For girls: *Y'simeich Eloh-him k'sara rivkah rachel v'lei-ah.*

Continue: *Y'varech'cha Adohnai, v'yishm'rehcha.*
             Ya-eir Adohnai panav eilehcha, viychunehka.
             Yisa Adohnai panav eilehcha, v'yaseim l'cha shalohm.

FRIDAY NIGHT *KIDDUSH*

Vay'hiy erev, vay'hiy vohker, yohm hashishiy.
Vay'chulu hashamayim v'ha-aretz v'chol tz'va-am.
Vay'chal Eloh-him bayohm hash'vi-iy, m'lachtoh asher asah.
Vayishboht bayohm hash'vi-iy mikkol m'lachtoh asher asah.
Vay'varech Eloh-him et yohm hash'vi-iy vay'kadeish oh-toh.
Kiy voh shavat mikkol m'lachtoh asher bara Eloh-him la-asoht.
Baruch attah Adohnai, Eloh-heinu melech ha-ohlam,
Bohrei p'riy hagafen.
Baruch attah Adohnai, Eloh-heinu melech ha-ohlam,
Asher kidshanu b'mitzvohtav v'ratza vanu,
V'shabat kodshoh b'ahavah uv'ratzohn hinchilanu,
Zikarohn l'ma-asei v'reishit.
Kiy hu yohm t'chilah l'mikra-ei kohdesh,
Zeicher liytzi-at mitzrayim.
Kiy vanu vacharta, v'ohtanu kidashta mikkol ha-amim,
V'shabbat kodsh'chah b'ahavah uv'ratzohn hinchaltanu.
Baruch attah Adohnai, m'kaddeish hashabbat.

SELECTION FROM THE *SHABBAT* MORNING SERVICE

FOR WASHING OF HANDS AND BODILY FUNCTIONS:

Baruch attah Adohnai, Eloh-heinu, melech ha-ohlam,
asher kidshanu b'mitzvohtav, v'tzivanu, al n'tilat yadayim.
Baruch attah Adohnai, Eloh-heinu melech ha-ohlam,
Asher yatzar et ha-adam b'chochmah
Uvara voh n'kavim n'kavim chalulim chalulim.
Galu-iy v'yadu-a lifnei chisei ch'voh-decha She-im yipatei-ach echad meihem
Oh yisateim echad meihem iy efshar l'hitkayeim
V'la-amohd l'fanehcha. Baruch attah Adohnai,
rohfei chol basar, umaffiy la-asoht.

OVER THE *TORAH*:

> *Baruch attah Adohnai, Eloh-heinu, melech ha-ohlam,*
> *Asher kidshanu b'mitzvohtav, v'tzivanu, la-asohk b'divrei Tohrah.*

> *V'ha-arev na, Adohnai Eloh-heinu, et divrei Tohrat'chah b'fiynu*
> *Uv'fiy amcha beit Yisra-eil. V'nih'yeh anachnu, v'tzeh-etza-einu,*
> *V'tzeh-etza-ei amchah beit Yisra-eil*
> *Kulanu yohd'ei sh'mehcha, v'lohmdei Tohratehcha.*
> *Baruch attah Adohnai,*
> *ham'lameid Tohrah l'ammoh Yisra-eil.*

> *Baruch attah Adohnai, Eloh-heinu, melech ha-ohlam,*
> *Asher bachar banu mikkol ha-amim, v'natan lanu et Tohratoh.*
> *Baruch attah Adohnai,*
> *nohtein haTohrah.*

THE PRIESTLY BLESSING:

> *Y'varech'cha Adohnai, v'yishm'rehcha.*
> *Ya-eir Adohnai panav, eilehcha, viychunehka.*
> *Yisa Adohnai panav eilehcha, v'yaseim l'cha shalohm.*

(Recite here the Morning Blessings, pages 144 to 145.)

RECALLING THE BIBLICALLY-PRESCRIBED *SHABBAT* SACRIFICE:

> *Uv'yohm hashabbat, sh'nei ch'vasim b'nei shanah t'mimim;*
> *ush'nei esrohnim sohlet minchah b'lulah vashemen v'niskoh.*
> *Ohlat Shabbat b'shabbatoh,*
> *al ohlat hatamid v'niskah.*

Recite *Ashrei*, page 147.

EIL ADOHN

(Note: the initial letters of the lines form the *Alef-Bet* .)

Eil adohn, al kol hama-asim,
Baruch um'vohrach, b'fiy kol n'shamah,
Godloh v'tuvoh malei ohlam,
Da-at ut'vunah sohvavim ohttoh.
Hamitga-eh al chayyoht hakohdesh,
V'nehdar b'chavohd al hamerkavah,
Z'chut umiyshohr lif'nei chisoh,
Chesed v'rachamim lifnei ch'vohdoh.
Tohvim m'ohroht shebara Eloh-heinu,
Y'tzaram b'da-at, b'viynah uv'haskeil,
Koh-ach ugvurah natan bahem,
Lih'yoht mohshlim b'kerev teiveil.
M'lei-im ziv, um'fiykiym nohgah,
Na-eh ziyvam b'chol ha-ohlam,
S'meichim b'tzeitam, v'sasim b'voh-am,
Ohsim b'eimah, r'tzohn kohnam.
P'eir v'chavohd nohtnim lishmoh,
TZahohlah v'rinah, l'zeicher malchutoh,
Kara lashemesh, vayizrach ohr,
Ra-ah v'hitkin, tzurat hal'vanah.
Shevach nohtnim loh, kol tz'vah marohm.
Tiferet ug'dulah, s'rafim v'ohfanim, v'chayoht hakohdesh.

THE *SHEMA*

(See pages 148 to 149.).

165

THE *AMIDAH*

First three blessings:

(*See page 150*)

Fourth blessing:

(Instead of the fourth blessing for Friday night, recite the following:)

> *Yismach mohsheh b'matnat chelkoh, Kiy eved neh-ehman karata loh.*
> *K'lil tiferet b'rohshoh natata, B'omdoh l'fanehcha al har sinai;*
> *Ush'nei luchoht avanim hohrid b'yadoh,*
> *V'chatuv bahem sh'mirat shabbat.*
> *V'chein katuv b'Tohratehcha.*

Continue with *V'shamru* (page 160.)

Final blessing:

See above, pages 151 to 152.

THE READING OF THE LAW

The Opening of the Ark:

> *Vay'hiy binsoh-a ha-arohn, vayohmehr mohsheh,*
> *Kumah Adohhnai, v'yafutzu oyvehcha, V'yanusu m'sanehcha mipanehcha.*
> *Kiy mitziyohn, teitzei Tohrah, Ud'var Adohnai miyrushalayim.*
> *Baruch shenatan Tohrah l'ammoh Yisra-eil bikdushatoh.*

On taking out the Scrolls:

> *Sh'ma Yisra-eil, Adohnai Eloh-heinu, Adohnai echad.*
> *Echad Eloh-heinu, gadohl adohneinu, kadohsh sh'moh.*
> *Gadlu lAdohhnai ittiy, un'rohmamah sh'moh yachdav.*

Blessings on being called up to the Torah,

See above, page 152.

Hymn (psalm 29) for returning the Scrolls to the Ark:

Hohdoh al eretz v'shamayim, vayarem keren l'ammoh
T'hilah l'chol chasidav livnei Yisra-eil am k'rohvoh,
Hal'luyah, hal'luyah.

Mizmohr l'david:

Havu lAdohnai b'nei eilim Havu lAdohnai kavohd va-ohz.
Havu lAdohnai k'vohd sh'moh Hishtachavu lAdohnai b'hadrat kohdesh.
Kohl Adohnai al hamayim Eil hakavohd hirim Adohnai al mayim rabim.
Kohl Adohnai bakoh-ach kohl Adohnai behadar.
Kohl Adohnai shohveir arazim vay'shabeir Adohnai et arzei halvanohn.
Vayarkideim k'mmoh eigel l'vanohn v'siryohn k'mmoh ven r'eimim.
Kohl Adohnai chohtzeiv lahavoht eish.
Kohl Adohnai yachil midbar yachil Adohnai midbar kadeish.
Kohl Adohnai y'chohleil ayaloht vayechesohf y'aroht
Uv'heichaloh kuloh ohmeir kavohd.
Adohnai lamabul yashav vayeishev Adohnai melech l'ohlam.
Adohnai ohz l'ammoh yitein Adohnai y'vareich et ammoh vashalohm.

Verses sung after placing the Scrolls in the Ark:

Eitz chayyim hiy, lamachazikim bah, v'tohm'cheha m'ushar.
D'racheha darchei noh-am, v'chol n'tivoh-teha shalohm.
Hashiveinu Adohnai eilehcha v'nashuvah
Chadeish yameinu k'kedem.

SELECTION FROM THE SHABBAT ADDITIONAL SERVICE

THE *AMIDAH*

First three blessings:

See above, page 150.

Fourth blessing:

(Instead of the fourth blessing for Friday night, commence with:

Uv'yohm haShabbat

See above, page 164, and continue with:

> *Yism'chu v'malchut'cha shohmrei shabbat, v'kohrei ohneg.*
> *Am m'kadshei sh'vi-iy, kulam yisb'u v'yitangu mituvehcha,*
> *V'hash'vi-iy ratziyta boh v'kidashtoh.*
> *Chemdat yamim ohttoh karata zeicher l'ma-asei v'reishit*
>
> ... ...
>
> *Baruch attah Adohnai,*
> *m'kadeish hashabbat.*

Fifth blessing:

> *V'techezehna eineinu, b'shuv'cha l'tziyyohn b'rachamim.*
> *Baruch attah Adohnai,*
> *hamachazir sh'chinatoh l'tziyyohn.*

Sixth blessing:

> *V'chohl hachayyim yohducha selah*
> *viy'hallalu et shimcha be-emet.*
> *Ha-eil y'shu-ateinu v'ezrateinu, selah.*
> *Baruch attah Adohnai,*
> *hatohv shimcha, ul'cha na-eh l'hohdoht.*

For final (*Sim shalohm*) blessing, *see above, pages 151 to 152.*

168

EIN KELOH-HEINU

> *Ein keloh-heinu, ein kadohneinu,*
> *ein k'malkeinu, ein k'mohshi-einu.*
> *Miy cheiloh-heinu, miy chadohneinu,*
> *miy ch'malkeinu, miy ch'mohshi-einu.*
> *Nohdeh lehloh-heinu, nohdeh ladohneinu,*
> *nohdeh l'malkeinu, nohdeh l'mohshi-einu.*
> *Baruch eloh-heinu, baruch adohneinu,*
> *baruch malkeinu, baruch mohshi-einu.*
> *Attah hu eloh-heinu, attah hu adohneinu,*
> *attah hu malkeinu, attah hu mohshi-einu.*
> *Attah hu shehiktiyru, avohteinu l'fanehcha,*
> *et k'tohret hasamim.*

ALEINU

See above, page 153.

ANIM ZEMIROHT

This is chanted by Reader and congregation alternately. The Reader's line appears here in bold type.

> **Anim z'miroht v'shirim e-erohg,**
> **kiy eilehcha nafshi ta-arohg.**

> *Nafshi chimda b'tzeil yadehcha,*
> *lada-at kol raz sohdehcha.*

> **Miydei dabriy bichvohdehcha,**
> **hohmeh libbiy el dohdehcha.**

> *Al kein adabbeir b'cha nichbadoht,*
> *v'shimcha achabeid b'shirei y'didoht.*

> **Asapra k'vohdcha v'loh r'iytiycha,**
> **adamcha achancha v'loh y'datiycha.**

169

B'yad n'vi-ehcha b'sohd avadehcha,
dimiyta hadar k'vohd hohdehcha.

G'dulat'cha ugvuratehcha,
kinnu l'tohkef p'ulatehcha.

Dimmu oht'cha v'loh ch'fiy yeshcha,
vay'shavucha l'fiy ma-asehcha.

Himshilucha b'rohv chezyohnoht,
hincha echad b'chol dimyohnoht.

Vayechezu v'cha ziknah uvacharut,
us'ar rohshcha b'seivah v'shacharut.

Ziknah b'yohm din uvacharut b'yohm k'rav,
k'ish milchamoht yadav loh rav.

Chavash kohvah y'shu-a b'rohshoh,
hohshi-a loh y'miynoh, uzroh-a kodshoh.

Tall'lei ohroht, rohshoh nimla,
uk'vutzohtav r'sisei lailah.

Yitpa-eir biy kiy chafetz biy,
v'hu yih'yeh liy la-ateret tz'viy.

Ketem tahor paz d'mut rohshoh,
v'chak al metzach k'vohd sheim kodshoh.

L'chein ul'chavohd, tz'viy tif'arah,
ummatoh loh itrah atarah.

Machl'foht rohshoh k'viymei v'churoht,
k'vutzohtav taltalim sh'chohroht.

N'vei hatzedek tz'vi tif'artoh,
ya-aleh nah al rohsh simchatoh.

S'gulatoh t'hiy v'yadoh ateret,
utz'nif m'luchah, tz'vi tif'eret.

Amusim n'sa-am ateret indam,
mei-asher yakru b'einav kibdam.

P'eiroh alai uf'eiriy alav,
v'karohv eilai, b'kohriy eilav.

Tzach v'adohm lilvushoh adohm,
purah b'dorchoh b'voh-oh mei-edohm.

Kesher t'fillin herah l'anav,
t'munat Adohhnai l'neged einav.

Rohtzeh b'ammoh anavim y'fa-eir,
yohsheiv t'hilloht, bam l'hitpa-eir.

Rohsh d'varcha emet kohrei meirohsh,
dohr vadohr am dohreshcha d'rohsh.

Shit hamohn shirai nah alehcha,
v'rinatiy tikrav eilehcha.

T'hilatiy t'hiy l'rohsh'cha ateret,
ut'filatiy tikkohn k'tohret.

Tiykar Shirat rash b'einecha,
K'shir yushar al korbanehcha.

Birchatiy ta-aleh l'rohsh mashbir;
m'chohleil umohlid tzadik kabbir.

Uv'virchatiy t'na-anna liy rohsh,
v'ohttah kach l'cha kivsamim rohsh.

Ye-erav nah siychiy alehcha,
kiy nafshiy ta-arohg eilehcha.

The congregation repeats the last two lines

ADOHN OHLAM

> *Adohn ohlam, asher malach, b'terem kol y'tzir nivra.*
> *L'eit na-asah v'cheftzoh kohl, azai melech sh'moh nikra.*
> *V'acharei kichloht hakohl, l'vadoh yimlohch nohra.*
> *V'hu hayah, v'hu hohveh, v'hu yih'yeh, b'tifarah.*
> *V'hu echad, v'ein sheiniy l'hamshil loh l'hachbirah.*
> *B'liy reishit b'liy tachlit, v'loh ha-ohz v'hamisrah.*
> *V'hu eiliy, v'chai goh-aliy, v'tzur chevliy b'eit tzarah.*
> *V'hu nisiy umanohs liy, m'nat kohsiy b'yohm ekra.*
> *B'yadoh afkid ruchiy, b'eit iyshan v'a-iyrah.*
> *V'im ruchiy g'viy-atiy, Adohnai liy, v'loh iyra.*

SHABBAT KIDDUSH

Commence with: *Veshamru,*

See page 160.

Continue:

> *Al kein beirach Adohnai et yohm hashabbat,*
> *vay'kadsheihu.*
> *Baruch attah Adohnai, Eloh-heinu, melech ha-ohlam,*
> *bohrei p'riy hagafen.*

172

XX

Returning to Synagogue
After a Prolonged Absence

Although there may seem to be quite a few points listed below that you have to watch out for in advance of your return, do not worry. You will be warmly welcomed, and, if you ask for help, the regulars will be delighted to give it. If you are to be given a synagogue honour, you will also be guided clearly by the Wardens. The purpose of this section is merely to prepare you, and to try to set your mind at rest by outlining the most common synagogue scenarios.

The fact that you are reading this book means that you have the tools to help you follow the service. Revise well the chapter relating to the particular service you will be attending, to help clarify the order of the service and the synagogue practices and procedures.

If you are making a visit to a synagogue because something has occurred in your life which has prompted you to seek spiritual solace, it is vital that you gain the maximum benefit from your visit. It is particularly important to ensure that your unfamiliarity with the service does not add to your feelings of anxiety. You might consider arranging to visit the Rabbi beforehand, to share your problem with him, before proceeding, with his help, to a return to synagogue.

If you are returning to synagogue because of a happy event, such as a *Barmitzvah*, an *Aufruf* (the 'calling-up' of a bridegroom on the *Shabbat* before his wedding), or the naming of a baby girl, it would be as well to ascertain beforehand whether it is the intention of the Wardens to call you up, either for an *Aliyah* to the *Torah*, for *Hagbahah* or *G'lilah*, or to open the Ark (*P'tichah*). Remember, it is also customary to accord an honour to any visitor. That being the case, it would be advisable to familiarize yourself in good time with the guidance we have provided in this book, and, if you are to receive an honour, to inquire beforehand, of someone who knows your synagogue's procedures, as to exactly how you should discharge your task. Make sure you know your full Hebrew name, which includes that of your father (e.g. *Yitzchak ben Avraham* ('Isaac son of Abraham').

Returning to Synagogue After a Prolonged Absence

If you are in synagogue in order to have a prayer recited for a sick member of your family or a friend, then you will need to ascertain not only his or her Hebrew name, but also the Hebrew name of the sick person's mother. This is derived from King David who, when in trouble, cried out, "I am Thy Servant, the son of Thy *handmaid*". So the form of the name will be, for example, *Yitzchak ben Sarah* ('Isaac son of Sarah').

If you are not a regular attender, even if you are a long-standing member, it is conceivable that the Wardens may have forgotten precisely who you are, or that a younger Warden may not have made your acquaintance. Don't be offended, unless, that is, you yourself have a photographic memory which never lets you down on 'who's who?'. So, immediately on arrival at synagogue, approach the Wardens and introduce yourself. If you are in synagogue for a special anniversary, and would like to be 'called up' to the *Torah* reading, remind them of your wish.

Remember that, if you are attending an Evening Service, whether during the week or on Friday night, the congregation does not wear a *Tallit*. The one exception to this rule is *Kol Nidrei* night.

If you are to open or close the Ark, seek exact instructions as to the location of the curtain cord, whether you do both the opening and the closing, whether or not there are doors to close afterwards, and at what precise moment you are to open and close. Inquire also as to which side to descend from the Ark, with whom to shake hands on completing your *Mitzvah*, and which route to take back to your seat.

Some of the older synagogues have reserved seats, and the members who may have been sitting in those seats, and their fathers and grandfathers before them, for decades, occasionally get rather peeved if a stranger, arriving before them occupies their seat. (I don't suppose too many people would take kindly to a colleague suddenly occupying their desk at work without a 'by your leave'). To avoid the embarrassment of having to move, ascertain on arrival whether or not the seat you are proposing to occupy belongs to a regular member.

If you are joining a family for a celebration (*Barmitzvah, Aufruf,* etc.), ask the Warden, or a nearby worshipper, on arrival, where the '*simchah* party' is sitting. They will probably be occupying the front rows of the synagogue. Remember that the very front row will be for the immediate family. If you are not family, but a close friend, then choose somewhere along the second or third rows. You can always be invited to come forward. It is embarrassing, however, to be asked to move out of your seat so that a relative can take up his rightful place. Women should take note that this consideration also applies in the Ladies Gallery section.

Remember that when 'the congregation' is invited to *Kiddush* at the conclusion of the service, even if it is a celebratory *Kiddush* (for a *Barmitzvah*, wedding anniversary, etc.) this includes everyone present in synagogue, including visitors. Remember not to eat or drink before the *Kiddush* has been recited. Do not be shy. This is your opportunity to meet people. Introduce yourself to the Rabbi, and do not be afraid to engage him in discussion (preferably after having given him time to drink his whisky!) and to tell him whether you agreed or disagreed with his sermon! Talk also to whomever else is standing near you.

Return your *Tallit, Siddur* and *Chumash* after the service to the place where they are stored.

SPECIAL FORMS OF GREETING

There are certain greetings that we exchange with other congregants on special holy days, and particularly at the conclusion of the service on those occasions:

On *Shabbat* we say: *Shabbat shalom!*

At the termination of *Shabbat* we say: *Shavua tov* ('have a good week'). Some traditionalists prefer the old Yiddish greeting: *Gutt Voch.*

On festivals we say: *Chag same-ach.*

On *Rosh Hashanah* we say: *L'shanah tovah* ('for a good year'). Or, if you are ambitious, the longer form: *L'shanah tovah tikateiv (v'teichateim).* There are also feminine forms for addressing women, and plural forms for addressing a group. Don't worry though: if you just say *L'shanah tovah* to everyone, it will be very acceptable.

On attending a happy, life-cycle celebration we say *Mazal Tov.*

On meeting someone for the first time, or after a very prolonged interval,

On meeting someone for the first time, or after a very prolonged interval, we say: *Shalom aleichem.*

On wishing someone a speedy recovery, we say: *R'fu-ah sh'leimah.*

On greeting someone after they have completed a synagogue honour, we say: *Yishar kochacha* (normally contracted to *Yishkoach*).

On wishing someone 'Long Life' after they have suffered a bereavement, or when they are commemorating a *Yahrzeit*, we either use the English greeting or say: *Chayyim aruchim* or *Arichat Yamim.*

On drinking someone's health we say: *L'chayyim.*

* * * * * * * * * * * *

Afterword

On completing any Talmudic chapter, the student recites the words *hadran alach*, "we shall return to you". The implication is that, however deeply we have studied that chapter of Talmud, we are still well aware that we have only just scratched the surface, and left many insights undiscovered, which will necessitate future exploration.

I do not make any such claim for my book. There are no sub-texts or hidden layers of significance underlying it. It is merely a tool towards achieving greater familiarisation with the *Siddur*, which assuredly does possess those hidden spiritual, emotional and mystical layers.

My prayer is that my readers will, nevertheless, have learnt much about the liturgy from this book, and that they will have also been inspired thereby to recite *hadran alach* "we shall return to you", to deeper and more informed commitment and practice. I pray that they will continue their voyage of religious exploration and discovery, and proceed to the deeper study of our glorious heritage.

For Further Reading

Laws of Prayer, in *Code of Jewish Law (Kitzur Shulchan Aruch)*. Various translated editions.

Aryeh, I. and Dworkes, J. (eds.), *The Hafetz Hayyim on the Siddur*. Jerusalem, 1974.

Cohen, J.M., See list of publications on prayer at beginning of this book.

Eisenberg, P. and A., *The Story of the Prayer Book*. Hartford, Conn., 1968.

Elkins, D. Peretz, *Moments of Transcendence: Inspirational Readings for Rosh Hashanah and Yom Kippur* (two volumes). New Jersey, 1992.

Greenberg, S. (ed.), *A Treasury of Thoughts on Jewish Prayer*. New Jersey, 1995.

Heinemann, J., *Prayer in the Talmud*. Berlin, 1977.

Hertz, J. H., *The Authorized Daily Prayer Book*. London, 1947.

Jacobson, B.S., *Meditations on the Siddur*. Tel Aviv, 1966.

Jakobovits, I., *Journal of a Rabbi*. London, 1967.

Kirzner, Y. and Aiken, L., *The Art of Jewish Prayer*. New Jersey, 1996.

Kohn, A., *Prayer*. London, 1971.

Kohn, J., *The Synagogue in Jewish Life*. New York, 1973.

Munk, E., *The World of Prayer*. New York, 1963.

Nulman, M., *The Encyclopedia of Jewish Prayer*. New Jersey, 1995.

Petuchowski, J.J., *Understanding Jewish Prayer*. New York, 1972.

Reif, S., *Judaism and Hebrew Prayer*. Cambridge, 1993.

Schach, S., *The Structure of the Siddur*. New Jersey, 1996.

Weiss, A., *Women at Prayer*. New Jersey, 1990.

Index

Index

Index